Wrestling With God

A UNITARIAN UNIVERSALIST GUIDE

FOR

SKEPTICS AND BELIEVERS

Tom Owen-Towle

Cover Photograph:

The Hand of God by Carl Milles
1952-1954
127x67x41 cm

Human being, perched upon the ground of Being ("The Hand of God"), is portrayed as gazing upward into the vast, mysterious cosmos (this same sculpture was also called "The Universe")...wondering, exploring, stretching, even daring to call deity to account—wrestling with God.

Photograph taken by Tom Owen-Towle in Carl Milles Garden in Stockholm, Sweden (1968)

(paperback) 9 8 7 6 5 4 3 2 1

Wrestling With God
Copyright © 2002 by Tom Owen-Towle

The pages of this edition are printed on recycled paper.

FIRST EDITION / SECOND PRINTING, 2004

ISBN 0-9715421-1-2

Dedication

To all religious pilgrims who pitch tent in the creases between belief and skepticism, uncertainty and devotion...who willingly carry on a persistent lover's quarrel with God.

Table of Contents

Prologue

To believe in God is impossible—
not to believe in God is absurd.

—Voltaire

A conscience faithful till death is of more impor-
tance than being on a certain side, whether of belief
or unbelief.

—Michael Novak

My life-journey has been one extended wrestling match with God—evolving from an early mindless embrace to categorical rejection, then gradually yet resolutely proceeding toward my current status as a questioning believer or trustful agnostic. I have emerged a theological hybrid who chooses to juggle live paradoxes concerning the Holy. I am at peace with Walt Whitman's claim: "Do I contradict myself? Yes, I contain multitudes!" Probably innumerable Unitarian Universalists, when pressed, would admit to being religious mongrels.

The following abbreviated account of my lover's quarrel with the Eternal serves both as self-clarifier and as stimulus for the reader's reflections. After all, it's through keeping current with God that we invigorate our very humanity, since theology and anthropology are braided.

As a child I was swept off my feet by God. Although grounded in secure parental love, I bore a tenacious need to cling to an external power. My God was a kindly and patient Being, accompanying me wherever my youthful feet strode. I "used" the Almighty, whether praying with my girlfriend before necking sessions or currying divine favor before tough tests in the classroom and pivotal foul shots in basketball games. This symbiotic linkage served me fairly well from childhood through college.

My God-tie started to unravel in, of all places, theological school. For too long, I had been puffing up God's ego while belittling my own. As I started to shape my own identity, I began to doubt the bedrock, hitherto unassailable, attributes of God. Soon the services of a master potter grew less and less necessary.

I startled myself by writing virulent anti-God poems during my seminary career. I was predictably chastised by the Presbyterian church back home for my "death of God" writings in our theological school journal. To be sure, the 1960s were a revolutionary era of severe questioning, even among prominent theologians; nonetheless, I found myself dangling on a limb, still desiring to be a parish minister, yet possessing an increasingly shrinking faith in God and attendant doctrines. Mohammed always reminded his disciples: "Whoever knows God, stammers!" Well, we radical seminarians were stammering a lot, both privately and publicly.

Shortly after ordination in July 1967, I scrambled to discover a roomier tradition within which to ply my trade. Ministry was the wrong profession for fabrications or fantasies. A high level of congruence would prove essential, whether one was soothing the brow of the dying or "speaking the truth in love" to a clan of worshippers. So, I sought a house of faith where I could exemplify 90% integrity rather than 65%.

It was during this arduous night of the soul that I penned a lover's quarrel poem entitled *Even God*:

Even God gets tired of too much hallelujah

—Carl Sandburg

*It's bad enough to discover Yahweh fussing
and stomping around the celestial haunt,
encircled by angels strumming harps
and indolent humans gorging on grapes.*

Heaven is honeyed.

*God's dismay is intensified by the
Wafting chorus of interminable hallelujahs.*

*"Desist, O earthlings, be not insipid grovelers.
You were not created to mouth mindless praise,
Brown-nosing for parcels of eternity.
Rise up, my offspring, stand whole,
Dance your awe and roar your grievances
In full-spirited measure."*

In 1969, through intense reading combined with happenstance, I fell upon the spacious abode of Unitarian Universalism where one can believe critically about matters holy—indeed, where the treasures of atheism, agnosticism, and affirmatism (the three A's) were equally pondered in the church parlor. As a liberal religionist I could regain kinship with the Spirit, acknowledging that language about Transcendence is analogical, never literal, and that "claims about God proceed first of all from the soul" (Jung).

9

Thirty-five years later, I am still making periodic adjustments in my ever-maturing covenant with the Eternal One. However unorthodox my spiritual condition may appear to mainline scrutiny, I proudly reside in the middle realm, straddling the three A's simultaneously. My approach is akin to that of columnist Ellen Goodman who writes: "In an argument between true believers, I often side with ambivalence. I'm drawn to the ambidextrous American who can argue with both hands." I can neither explain adequately nor avoid entirely the presence of God. So I argue with both hands.

I have evolved into a creature willing to join the Jewish-inspired company of those who would "argue with heaven," calling deity to account. In short, my lover's quarrel with God has not, nor ever will, come to a halt.

Accordingly, I write this book as a midstream seafarer joyfully enmeshed in what poet Anne Sexton called "the awful rowing toward God." Rowing that demands full employment of the mental and spiritual oars at my disposal. Rowing sometimes alone, but most satisfyingly as a team member. Rowing both toward a destination and just for the fun of it.

Enough on the state of my god-quest. How goes it with yours? Moreover, what seems to be the disposition of our freethinking faith with respect to God? Without presuming to encapsulate the Unitarian Universalist theological mood, I would venture one observation. I presently detect a palpable enthusiasm (literally, "god-filledness") within our fold.

A couple decades ago when poet May Sarton addressed the Unitarian Church in Brattleboro, Vermont she remarked that "the kind, intelligent people gathered in a big room looking out on pine trees did not really want to think about God, His absence (many of my poems speak of that) or His presence." Sarton's pointed observation no longer holds true for Unitarian Universalism.

Newcomers are entering our gates nowadays hungry for spiritual affiliation and discipline. Unabashedly *homo religiosus*, seekers of the transcendent. As one member of our own congregation pined: "I originally came to First Church to seek God but quickly became occupied on various committees. I lost the time and energy to look for the Holy. It was a huge loss!" Parishioners are finding the time and urging the issue now— bursting forth from cocoons of theological shyness, apathy, or resistance.

Contemporary Unitarian Universalists stand ready to feed their spirits through doing theology: engaging in a form of mapmaking where the mystery of *theos* is represented by means of a *logos* or word picture. Congregants are choosing to become practicing theologians themselves rather than turn the job over to in-resident religious professionals.

Furthermore, witness the extensive interest concerning deity in our larger society. Steve Waldman, co-founder of *beliefnet.com*, remarking on the most popular topics on the Internet, says: "God is right up there with sex!" The same is true in the printed word as well, what with the spate of recent volumes ranging from the history of God to a biography of God to conversations with God. The best-selling author and psycho-spiritual coach, Deepak Chopra, has written a volume entitled *How to*

Know God: The Soul's Journey into the Mystery of Mysteries. In this latest and perhaps most ambitious work, Chopra explores seven ways we experience God.

Unquestionably, the Creator has been getting more ink today than in a long time...and oft from the unlikely pens of established physicists or adventurous literati. There even exists contemporary medical research that makes the case for a sixth human sense that intuitively perceives the divine. God may be on the human brain, declare some scientists. Perhaps we are hardwired to be religious seekers.

God is presumably bemused by the current avalanche of words about Him/Her/Itself. Is this theological fervor due to the arrival of the millennium, social unrest, spiritual appetite, psychic loneliness, or just what? There's undoubtedly a mix of reasons. In any case, we must be cautious never to confuse verbiage about God with proximity to God. *The Upanishads* (Hindu scriptures) send brash metaphysicians reeling when they caution: "Those who think that God is not comprehended, by them God is comprehended; but those who think that God is comprehended, know God not."

So, why more frail, even futile, soundings about God? Why another book? Well, at least this one's relatively short. A tiny book on a huge topic! I learned long ago to be brief—especially when writing about indescribable realities like love or God. Anyway, as Henry David Thoreau warned: "It takes a long time to write something short!"

Moreover, whereas there are plenty of books penned from the viewpoint of the believer and an adequate number by unbelievers, to my knowledge there is no volume that applauds critical piety, trustful uncertainty, and skeptical believing as complementary attitudes to juggle during the religious journey. Unitarian Universalism celebrates an unheralded yet distinct approach to the question of an Ultimate Being. Maybe God would welcome an unorthodox book from the bosom of a movement that has no trouble both doubting and affirming its very Being!

A follow-up reason for this book: "God" may well be what foremost 20th-century Jewish theologian Martin Buber called, "the most heavy-laden of all human words. None has become so soiled, so mutilated." Yet, instead of throwing in the towel and walking away, Buber urges us to uphold the struggle: "We cannot cleanse the word 'God' and we cannot make it whole; but defiled as it is, we can raise it from the ground and set it over an hour of great care." I agree. Unitarian Universalist believers and nonbelievers alike are charged to purify corrupted concepts such as God through a revisioning process that constitutes our duty and joy.

Additionally, I can't help myself. And I don't think I'm alone ensconced in creative disquiet. There's no idea that fascinates yet frustrates us creatures more than God. Our humanity is expanded, even ennobled, when we do hard-nosed scuffling with the Creator. Micah exhorts us to "Seek God and live" (5:4). Consequently, we struggle with God not so much to garner eternal reward as to relish abundant life...here and now.

Along with Jacob, the epitaph of countless Unitarian Universalists could gladly read: "You have wrestled with beings divine and human" (Genesis 32:29). We have been known to emerge from many a theological skirmish both limping and graced with a new name such as the one Jacob acquired, "Israel"—literally, "the one who struggles with God." Being a bona fide *godwrestler* definitely comprises a reputable pursuit and holy bargain. We freethinking mystics would second Simone Weil's sentiment: "One can never wrestle enough with God, if one does so out of pure regard for truth."

There is timeliness as well. We have entered a fresh century, and updating our perspectives on God will better equip us to lead fully religious, that is, fully human lives. We owe it to ourselves and ensuing generations to convey neither an expedient nor a befuddled theology but a complicatedly clear one.

Nothing will prove more harmful to civilization than humans fatheadedly pushing simplistic views about God and death, life and love. The modern epoch will demand our healthiest grasp, however flawed and unfinished, of the human-divine dynamic. As Meister Eckhart (1260-1327) reminds us: "God must be brought to birth in the soul again and again."

If God is a nonsensical and irrelevant concept for you, if you contend "God's in his heaven and all is right with world," or if you are complacent in your irresoluteness, then this book won't likely either reach your mind or sing to your soul.

On the other hand, if you consider yourself a critical (not true) and open-minded (not empty) seeker, and if you are willing to be jarred out of your comfy theological nest while soaring with paradoxes about the Eternal, then *Wrestling With God* might just furnish sustenance for the strenuous days and nights of your sojourn.

I. RIDERS OF PARADOXES

I have learned to make my mind large, as the universe is large, so that there can be room for paradoxes.

—Maxine Hong Kingston

If I used the word God this week, I don't commit myself to use it next week. Nor do I contradict myself if, late the same Sunday, I say gods or Void or Goddess or (that old humanist standby) Spirit of Life.

—Daniel Hotchkiss

Being riders of paradoxes is apparently our peculiar niche as liberal religionists. We seem to pitch tent in the creases between mysticism and humanism, theism and naturalism, believing and doubting, devotion and skepticism. At our truest, Unitarian Universalists are spiritually ambidextrous, defining ourselves both from below and above. We are a reasonable religion with mystical sensibilities—in short, we are theological crossbreeds. Colleague Frances West puts it sagely: "The humanist and the theist live in me, each sometimes puzzled by the presence of the other, but willing to keep talking. So may it continue."

Clearly, there's a danger in either extreme. Arid humanism can trap us in the mundane and material, making us oblivious to transrational (note I didn't say irrational) nudges. On the other hand, unbridled theism can swallow humans in the supernal ether, when our paramount job is to make this precious earth more beautiful and just.

So, god-fearing or mystical humanism (what someone has awkwardly coined "humanisticism") is perhaps the principal ambiguity Unitarian Universalists must harness, then ride. Some do it sidesaddle, tentatively; others with both hands to the reins, galloping full-bore ahead. Regardless, it provides a spirited jaunt!

There are numerous ways of illustrating our theological hybridism as freethinking mystics with hands. A couple of examples.

In the newspaper recently there was a report touting the medicinal value of prayer based on research conducted at the Heart Institute in Kansas City. The results were published in a respected medical journal. Overall, patients who were prayed for did 11% better than the patients in the control group, based on an evaluation of 35 medical measurements. And it should be noted that those praying and the patients did not know one another.

Now, as Unitarian Universalists, we use prayer primarily to center our own spiritual state rather than to reap specific rewards. But here's the other side of the paradox: as mystical humanists, we refuse to be stunned by any scientific study that proves the medicinal value of prayer. Why? Because our spirits sit wide open to mysteries beyond our creation and blessings beyond our prediction. And, in the name of human compassion, we regularly hold fellow kin tight in our prayerful thought.

Let me offer another example, rather homely yet poignant, that signals our Unitarian Universalist commitment to straddling the known and the unknown, science and mystery. It occurred early in the tenure of my ministry in Davenport, Iowa. During the course of every church year, I would meet individually with our first and second graders. Each child and I would engage in personal conversation, in which I would first recount what I found meaningful in my life and then relate why I attended church—and being the paid minister didn't qualify as sufficient reason.

I then asked each of these youngsters what was exciting or enjoyable in their daily lives. They would say things like "Mom and Dad, Christmas and soccer, friends and reading alone in their bedroom, camping under the stars and building stuff." And much more, straight from their bursting hearts.

My wee buddy, Adam Burke, mentioned two things that stood out in his life up to that point: "Dinosaurs and magic." Now, without overtheologizing this second grader's response, I like to think that Adam's passions pointed to something of earth and heaven, the familiar and the mysterious. Dinosaurs and magic. Adam was drawn to both realities, and so are we adults.

I painted the particular words of every child on stones that I had gathered from the Mississippi River region, then, in a simple ceremony, presented the engraved rocks to each as a gift. Twenty-five years later our paths crossed again in San Diego, where Adam was serving as the best man at his sister Abby's wedding, which I was conducting. After the service, when Adam was signing the marriage license, he nonchalantly reached down into his tuxedo pocket and pulled out his cherished rock and said: "Tom, this stone still sits on my bed stand, wherever I live, reminding me both of our Quad Cities

Church and our conversation together. And you know what? Dinosaurs and magic—or some version thereof—are still among my favorite things!"

And so, we Unitarian Universalists, of all ages and sizes, are summoned to be riders of paradoxes, to be fully rational and fully spiritual and fully compassionate—utterly open to the dinosaurs and magic that cross our path! We opt to be doggedly maturing rather than dogmatically secure pilgrims. We heed Ezekiel's imperative to "go up into the gaps." We deem it not merely tolerable, but desirable, as spiritual nonconformists to live well amidst the intractable doubts and nasty confusions at the heart of Reality.

Speaking of gaps, I'm reminded of our family excursion to the Sistine Chapel in Rome over a decade ago. My mind's eye is still riveted upon the dazzling panel in Michelangelo's ceiling mural depicting Adam and God. Adam raises an arm in the direction of the Infinite One, whose extremity, in turn, stabs down toward the dewy creature. Index fingers on both hands reach toward the other but do not touch. Everything trembles in midair between these outstretched fingers of humanity and divinity tirelessly striving to connect. And so it goes. In that zone where we reach but do not ultimately grasp one another is precisely where the bulk of our religious life is carried out...where the paradox of mystical humanism is ridden.

Who really wants existence tidily wrapped up? Who covets convictions set in stone? Plenty of people to be sure, but not Unitarian Universalists. Being mongrels isn't a dire position of last resort but our first choice. It's the way we choose to walk and talk, live and die during our sojourn on this planet. It's the way we do religion.

Church historian Earl Morse Wilbur relates a watershed moment for the Unitarian Ministerial Conference at Cincinnati in 1886 when arguments were aired on both sides as to whether atheists and agnostics should be embraced within our ranks. The Conference agreed by a substantial majority that "the Western Unitarian Conference conditions its fellowship on no dogmatic tests, but welcomes all who wish to join it to help establish Truth and Righteousness and Love in the World."

And when we examine the credentials of the signers of the Humanist Manifesto back in 1933, two things are discernible. First, most of the 34 were card-carrying Unitarian and/or Universalist ministers. Second, while the designers were neither secularists nor supernaturalists, they exuded an obvious fondness for the sacred. Unlike the orthodox theists of their day, they didn't worship an omnipotent, patriarchal figure high in the sky. Nonetheless, they were notably reverent travelers. They handled holy things with feeling. They were utterly open to the divine circulating through this earthly trek.

These thorough-going humanists talked of God, comfortably so, but in collaborative, naturalistic terms. They considered some sort of partnership between heaven and earth to be our supreme summons. As Burdette Backus put it:

> *Whenever we are helping humanity to be at its best, we are worshipping God...we are the children of a creative and dynamic universe, and its restless energy*

is at work within us to carry forward the work of creation. This is something of what I mean when I say that I believe in God...God is not an idea to be believed in; God is work to be done in the world. This work is being accomplished in the growth of human souls, yours and mine.

Such pacesetters struggled to extend religion beyond narrow humanism and doctrinaire theism. They were both hard-headed and soft-hearted theologians, refusing to harm anyone with their view of either humanity or divinity. They were seekers who were agile whether meditating upon the heavens or protesting earthly wrongs. I like to think of them as mystical or god-fearing humanists.

This reminds me of the humorous story of two men, Schwartz and Rosen, who are strolling to synagogue. Someone stops them and asks Rosen, "Why are you going to synagogue? Schwartz is a believer—I know why he's going. But you're not religious!" Rosen answers, "Well, Schwartz goes to talk to God, and I go to talk to Schwartz." You see, a full-fledged, hearty religion includes both human conversation and divine communion, an intriguing mix of Schwartz and Rosen.

Standing tall in our proud lineage of theological diversity, a contemporary Unitarian Universalist has mused: "I first entered Unitarian Universalism as a Christian, evolved into a religious humanist, and now am a card-carrying pagan—and I have never been asked to leave the fold!" Freethinking minister, Bruce Bode, seconds this motion:

With respect to an image of God, we can be theist, deist, polytheist, pantheist, atheist, and agnostic all at once. There can be something in each perspective that speaks to us and carries a truth for us. At one time we may lean more in one direction, and at another time in another...More than one spirit can live in us at once. A principle of complementary perspectives, and a willingness to live with paradox and even flat-out contradiction, can help to keep us alive and open to this beautiful, terrible world in which we live.

Such amplitude of conviction is shunned by mainline American religion, where clear-cut, often rigid, barriers separate the devotee from the cynic from the unknower. Spiritual seekers are arbitrarily pressured into claiming but one of these three positions. Such a procrustean squeeze is oversimplified. As Unitarian ancestor Justice Oliver Wendell Holmes exclaimed: "I would not give a fig for the simplicity this side of complexity, but I would give my life for the simplicity on the other side of complexity."

It's hard to avoid tokens of the Almighty on our streets and highways these days. Billboards bearing "messages from God" have appeared in some 40 states. These one-liners were commissioned anonymously and promote pithy theologisms, each signed simply "God":

—Will the road you're on get you to my place?

—Need a marriage counselor? I'm available.

—Keep using my name in vain, I'll make rush hour longer.

23

—I don't question your existence.

—Don't make me come down there.

Such a consumerized approach to spirituality may be a sincere advertising campaign to reach those who have drifted away from mainline religion, but "quickie" messages are too flippant and depthless for Unitarian Universalist taste.

In contrast to two recent books, *God Made Easy* and *Shortcuts to God*, we aver that faith is anything but "easy" and are wary of any earthling who would advise "shortcuts" to the Eternal One. As Alan Watts warns: despite our grandest human efforts, it remains impossible to "eff the ineffable."

We who willingly choose life's arduous path resonate with the religious struggle depicted in J. D. Salinger's novel, *Franny and Zooey:*

> *I don't want you to go away with the impression that there's any—you know— any inconvenience involved in the religious life. I mean a lot of people don't take it up just because they think it's going to involve a certain amount of nasty application and perseverance—you know what I mean?...As soon as we get out of chapel here, I hope you'll accept from me a little volume I've always admired,* **God Is My Hobby.**

Alas, God ought never be the subject of a casual topic or considered just another hobby. God-talk is an adventure to be undertaken seriously, albeit never grimly. I identify with the minister who recalls an interview she had with a pulpit search committee. "Are you a humanist or a theist?" someone probed. "Well, that all depends," she replied. "If a congregant is an inflexible humanist, then I enter the dialogue as a theist. And if they're a smug theist, then I'm a card-carrying humanist. I'm honorably ambidextrous!" She was rightly declaring that the minister's teaching function, in large measure, is to rattle comfort cages—to keep raising the questions with which parishioners must continually wrestle.

We religious professionals aren't worth much if we can't occasionally be effective banana peels: lying in wait, tripping people up, and knocking their spirits against novel perspectives. Catalysts for creative collisions.

As one iconoclastic observer astutely noted: "You will be interested in God's existence only if, in advance of proof, you care about the subject. And that depends on more than mere existence. After all, what does it matter to you if I can prove that lobsters exist, if you don't like lobsters?" That being the case, our job as clergy, as well as laity, is to work up an appetite for lobsters in our congregations from time to time.

Religion, at its most genuine, extends minds into shapes beyond either our imagining or our contentment. Countless theologians (and all who philosophize about God qualify as "students of God") resonate with Elie Wiesel's assertion: "One can be a good Jew, or a good Christian, with God or against God, but not without God. I quarrel with, fight with, and make up with God, but I am never without God." Doing theology is definitely a confounding discipline, not for the faint of heart or stiff of mind.

Ruefully, contemporary religious thought is all too frequently polarized among doctrinaire persuasions. But our founders knew otherwise; they practiced religious freedom and inclusion. Hence, America would prudently return to its rootedness in pluralism where seekers along the entire continuum between humanism and theism are not only tolerated but celebrated.

Our culture yearns for individuals who are theologically ambidextrous, able to argue authentically out of both sides of the soul, reflecting the attitude of our forebear Ralph Waldo Emerson: "If you believe, suspend your belief. If you doubt, take a leap of faith!" Such is the curious destiny of the liberal religious heritage we claim as Unitarian Universalists.

Blaise Pascal—an eminent 17th-century apologist for the Christian religion, as well as a mathematician and an experimental scientist—divided humankind into three groups: (1) those who know God and love him; (2) those who do not know God but seek him; and (3) those who neither know God nor seek him. The issue of God's gender aside, these distinctions roughly represent the categories of affirmatist, agnostic, and atheist. It's the manifest strength of Unitarian Universalism that, within our theological embrace, adherents can honestly assume all three positions at different junctures in their journey, or even concurrently, and still be considered an honorable religious quester.

When the three A's (atheism, agnosticism, and affirmatism) are clasped in resourceful tension, one's religious identity becomes hale and hearty—for each attitude brings a valuable gift to the theological table, providing a system of checks and balances. Blaise

Pascal noted as much in his confessional volume, Pensees:

> *Denying, believing and doubting completely are to humans what running is to a horse.*

Atheism is a purifying influence, eliminating obsolete or abhorrent renditions of the divine. Eminent 20th-century religious philosopher Abraham Heschel routinely mused that true prophets spend the bulk of their time interfering with and raging against puerile notions of the Creator.

Agnosticism supplies the essential gift of measured indecision, challenging earthlings to handle the sacred lightly without forcing it into formulas, to "live in the questions" (Rilke), rather than yielding to either certitude or apathy.

Affirmatism unflinchingly insists upon the inherent sacredness of existence, announcing "the lurking-places of God" (Thoreau), especially surprising locales of holy portent.

Blake's admonition obtains: "Without contraries, there is no progression." Healthy atheism produces a more inventive agnostic, while affirmatism impels us to be more supple atheists and agnostics. Holding paradoxes in sincere stretch keeps both suspicious and gullible proclivities from running amok. Alas, when theologically uptight, we are likely to "make premature peace" with either our ignorance or biases.

While entertaining the singular wisdom of all three approaches, Unitarian Universalists proceed cautiously along the soulful journey, for each interpretation harbors its own shadows as well. The atheist is susceptible to hollowness of soul and horizon. The agnostic is vulnerable to disinterest or "the brutality of indiscriminate skepticism" (Unitarian Herman Melville). The affirmatist can unwittingly become a sanctimonious crusader.

Caution is the better part of wisdom. Therefore, tread the sacred path, my fellow pilgrims, reverently and with eyes wide open!

II. ATHEISM: A CRITICAL ROLE

The atheist who lives with real interior courage is intrinsically better than a sniveling believer forever crying for help from an avuncular Deity.

—Geddes MacGregor

I am an atheist. I do not believe in God. Never did. But there is more. I also love God. I am an atheist who loves God...the word God serves as a symbol, a focus for the thoughts, feelings, and intuitions that go into our intimate, inward relation with the whole of reality, both known and unknown, seen and unseen.

—Alexie Crane

In our lover's quarrel with God, Unitarian Universalists appropriate what is salutary and helpful in the atheist critique. I start with something of a laundry list of atheistic postures so that the reader might land upon a perspective, or several, most in alignment with her/his own thinking.

We have all known *devoted* atheists, those individuals who splurge more effort debunking god than some believers do celebrating Him/Her/It. Peter Christiansen good-naturedly lampoons this group: "I tend to be wary of 'professional atheists'. They spend a little too much time thinking about God."

Then there are the *distracted* atheists: those people who don't have the time to waste on god-talk.

Another batch consists of what one might label *functional* atheists. These are individuals who sit in church or temple pews, going through rituals and mouthing doctrines, yet harboring in their hearts, and displaying in daily life, scant acknowledgment of a divine companion. These folks live as if God doesn't exist. They are, for practical purposes, disguised unbelievers.

A further distinction might be drawn. *Hopeful* atheists emphasize human freedom and potential. They gravitate toward secular humanism and occasionally embrace a naturalistic or mystical worldview. These pilgrims leave metaphysical speculation to others, while focusing on human-sized projects at hand—such as making a living, learning to love, preparing the way for future generations.

Cheerful atheists live confidently and comfortably a-theos—*without* but not *against* the notion of deity. They harbor no belief rather than disbelief. They are more accurately termed nontheists than atheists. In any case, these seekers are essentially at peace, both spiritually and socially, living void of metaphysical reference.

Unitarian Universalism is one established faith that contends that religious people can be self-ascribed atheists. We know that countless human explorers, within and without our fold, have experienced what they would call transcendent insights and moments without attributing them to a supernatural source. They perceive such encounters to be indigenous and natural to this earthly sphere.

Elsewhere on the continuum reside *pessimistic* atheists who stress human forlornness in an impersonal, even hostile, universe. Such nonbelievers have frequently grown up with tormented and twisted ties with God. Some are not merely skeptical but downright cynical and categorically rebuff anything divine. They grow queasy whenever the supernatural is cited.

Some, but not all, atheists are tinged with a sort of existential regret or even lostness. In fact, psychologist Paul Vitz studied the lives of several atheists and concluded that the bulk of them had lousy relationships with their fathers. Some even wanted to kill their dads. Undoubtedly, there is truth in Vitz's analysis, since rejection by one's earthly father often indicates disconnection from a heavenly patriarch as well.

However, one could clearly find agnostics and affirmatists who have also harbored troubled alliances with their fathers...or their mothers. I have counseled rabid believers who have felt the overweening urge to turn their lives over to an omnipotent, custodial sort of Being precisely because they suffered deficient parenting during formative years. In sum, we are our histories, and whereas our theologies frequently mirror our psycho-social development, our resultant conditions are varied and seldom easy to pigeonhole.

Colleague Clarke Wells draws yet another fruitful distinction between the atheist who rejects "the several idols of human invention, searching for a truth beyond them" *and* the variety who "are insensitive to the holy things of life and treats them accordingly." The first kind of atheist, claims Wells, and I would agree, seems to fit nicely in most of our Unitarian Universalist societies, while the second species has to reach some— accepting, as Wells puts it, "our custom of treating life as majestically holy and our handling of it with religious feeling."

This analysis seems to mesh with Paul Tillich's assessment: "If you can say in complete seriousness that life itself is shallow, then you are an atheist; but otherwise you are not. They who know about depth know about God." In any case, atheists endowed with a modicum of sacred consciousness tend to feel most at home in our liberal religious environs.

Throughout our sweep of history, Unitarian Universalists have sincerely wrestled with one or another of the aforementioned atheistic positions. My objective is to challenge our membership to refine and update our relationship to "atheism" in order to exhibit an honest faith. So I ask you, my fellow Unitarian Universalist sojourner, what version of atheism most informs your spiritual voyage?

It's tempting to settle for an outmoded, albeit comfortable, grasp of atheism, agnosticism, or affirmatism in our quests. Hence, the charge of this book remains to keep us awake, off-balance, current yet evolving.

I want to say more about the kind of atheism dedicated to repudiating jealous and vengeful deities. Even early Christians were persecuted as *atheoi* because they resisted the public veneration of the state gods. And centuries later a Jewish court convicted the notable Jewish religious philosopher, Spinoza, of atheism. His teachings were restricted and his writings banned. Throughout the sweep of the Western world, adherents have been tagged infidels because they disbelieved in the Gods of the ruling powers. Jews, Christians, and Muslims were all penalized as atheists, at one time or another in their respective histories, precisely because of such heretical views of divinity.

This was also the case with our mid-19th-century Universalist forebear, Abner Kneeland, who railed against the accepted Christian doctrines of his stodgy Boston cohorts. Although clearly an affirmer of God, he was branded an atheist because of the unorthodoxy of his perspective. Listen to Kneeland's own words:

> *I had no occasion to deny that there is a God; I believe that the whole universe is nature, and that God and nature are synonymous terms. I believe in a God that embraces all power, wisdom, justice, and goodness. Everything is God. I am not an atheist, but a pantheist.*

How quickly orthodox religionists have castigated those who have believed differently as nonbelievers and atheists. Heretics, literally "choice-makers" (a most principled station in our brand of religion), have been mercilessly crucified as infidels, apostates, backsliders, and miscreants.

Religious maverick Alan Watts had a marvelous phrase for the torching of straw gods. He called it "atheism in the name of God": an unabashed attempt to debunk any god-cepts that seemed either improbable or hideous. A continual purification of Gods that suspend the laws of nature. Provincial or petty gods. Gods that play favorites among teams or races or nations of the world. Gods who are supposedly responsible for premature deaths or crippling of children or cosmic catastrophes. As Emerson well noted, "Heartily know, when half-gods go, the gods arrive." One of the functions of mature religion, then, is to cleanse the temple of destructive, worn-out deities that more sensible ones might become apparent.

It matters what ideas of ultimacy we decide to reject. *Via negativa* has been an oft-utilized implement in the knapsack of world religions. Former president of the Unitarian Universalist Association, John Buehrens, relates the following exchange:

> *One person was speaking to another about religious matters. She said, "I don't believe in god. I'm an atheist." The listener responded, "Tell me what god it is that you don't believe in. I may reject it as well."*

And even when we don't deny the existence of certain deities we may dispute their manner of behavior. Atheists take seriously the critical truthfulness of one of religion's relentless questers, Job, in the Old Testament, who said:

> *Will you speak unjustly on God's behalf?*
> *Will you speak deceitfully for Him?*
> *What will happen when God examines you?*
> *Will you fool God as one fools humans?*

> —Job 13: 7-9

Job's buddies were worried that he was unduly critical of the divine and that there would be a harsh payment to come, as if Job hadn't already suffered enough. But Job held firm, feeling that any deity worth its salt should welcome human candor over mindless veneration.

Unitarian Universalism would submit that the Creator/Creation delights in earnest atheists who labor to rid the globe of intellectual laziness, emotional immaturity, and moral delinquency. Meister Eckhart felt that "our last and highest leave-taking is leaving God for God," and, furthermore, that "God is not found in the soul by adding anything but by a process of subtraction."

Mature atheism is represented by the "neti, neti" of Hindu theology meaning: "Not this! Not this!" Such skeptics do the dirty work of shedding debilitating images of divinity—work that idealists and romantic mystics seldom risk. Pruning is the critical method of the compassionate pilgrim.

I personally find atheism most valuable as a clarifying, cleansing vehicle and least useful when stubborn or combative. *Protest* marks a noteworthy heritage that not only rejects certain viewpoints but, moreover, "testifies on behalf of" what we hold to be true. Atheism is beneficial when employed in service of religious wisdom rather than as an outright negation of it.

Finally, being an honest atheist places one in good company. There are clearly nontheistic as well as theistic strands of Hinduism. Such questers are also consonant with the philosophy of Theravada Buddhism, one of the major world religions, where there exists no single, uniform concept of a personal deity; instead, a sense of the sacred permeates our moral actions. Buddha himself warned that ethereal speculation about the nature of deity or an afterlife not only was futile but also tended not to edification. And as for the Zen Buddhists, when one famous Roshi was asked, "What does Zen say about God," he remained silent.

The high religions of Asia do not acknowledge a personal absolute, yet consider the world to be unmistakably numinous. In China, Confucianism is essentially atheistic in that it concentrates on rules of behavior for the conduct of human life but has little to say about deity as a personal entity. It challenges earthlings to live in harmony with the way of heaven and duty rather than worship a supernal being.

Jainism, another great religion born in India, possesses no notion of a creator god, yet remains an uncommonly ethical faith, whose aspiration is to free the soul from bondage to matter through ascetic discipline.

Atheism at its healthiest, dare I say, at its holiest, provides a critical, purifying role in the pursuit of reasonable religion.

III. AGNOSTICISM: A DEFINITE MAYBE

The Tao that can be told is not the eternal Tao.
The name that can be named is not the eternal
Name.

—Lao-Tzu

I do not say there is no God. I do not know. As I told
you before, I have traveled very little. Only in this
world! The clergy know, I know, that they know that
they do not know!

—Robert Ingersoll

Honest agnosticism is a mark of reverence.

—David Rhys Williams

Faith and doubt both are needed—not as
antagonists but working side by side—to take us
around the unknown curve.

—Lillian Smith

The term agnostic is fairly new, first used in 1869 by the famous English biologist, Thomas Huxley, who remained a fervent religious follower throughout the course of his agnosticism. He phrased it as follows:

> *When I reached intellectual maturity and*
> *began to ask myself whether I was an*
> *atheist, a theist, or a pantheist...I found*
> *that the more I learned and reflected, the*
> *less ready was the answer....Others were*
> *quite sure they had attained a certain*
> *"gnosis,"—had more or less*
> *successfully, solved the problem of*
> *existence; while I was quite sure I had*

not, and had a pretty strong conviction that the problem was insoluble...

Agnosticism, in fact, is not a creed, but a method, the essence of which lies in the rigorous application of a single principle. That principle is of great antiquity...the axiom that every one should be able to give a reason for the faith that is in them...the fundamental axiom of modern science...In matters of the intellect, follow your reason as far as it will take you, without regard to any other consideration.

Agnosticism—the permanent suspension of belief based on incomplete knowledge—signals the human condition. We can't escape the existential state of partial wisdom. Certitude will never be within our grasp. "A definite maybe" was the phrase cartoonist Walt Kelly used when answering what he considered the really big questions. And comedienne Gilda Radner talked about life's "delicious ambiguity."

Yet the populous at large remains oft-confused or unresponsive to the integrity of the agnostic's perspective. Philosopher Bertrand Russell illustrates this plight in a telling anecdote during the process of his refusal to enter military conscription.

"When I reported to the prison warden," Russell said, his eyes changing from their objective gravity to a twinkle, "he asked me the customary questions—name, age, place of residence. Then he inquired, 'Religious affiliation?'

'Agnostic,' Russell replied. The poor man looked up, 'How do you spell that?' Russell spelled *'a-g-n-o-s-t-i-c'* for him. The warden wrote the word carefully on the prison admission form, then sighed, 'Oh, well; there are a great many sects nowadays, but I suppose we all worship the same God!'" Such ignorance surrounding frankly held qualms about God remains rampant to this day.

Notwithstanding, agnosticism constitutes a virtuous position held by reflective thinkers ranging from philosopher Sidney Hook, who claims to be an "unredeemed, skeptical God-seeker," to Protestant theologian Leslie Weatherhead, who wrote a book in 1965 entitled *The Christian Agnostic*, in which he forthrightly explored "God and our guesses."

In many ways, agnosticism has become a distinctive form of modern unbelief—reflective of our Unitarian Universalist *weltanschauung,* as evident in the words of minister Stephan Papa:

> *I call myself a mystical agnostic because even though we cannot know about a creator or sustainer, we do know, I believe, that the proper response to the miracle of existence is wonder, awe, worship, allegiance. So I append the word mystical. On the intellectual level, I am an agnostic; on the emotional, a mystic. Will I ever be whole? Will I ever know? Probably not.*

Yes, countless freethinkers could readily own the label "mystical agnostics." For ours is a faith that is filled with doubts, even as it proffers bountiful affirmations. The key test is to display healthful rather than debilitating doubt. There are important distinctions outlined by Unitarian Universalist Charles McGehee, who classifies six brands of doubt: honest, necessary, creative, destructive, immortal, and lonely doubt. He further pens: "In facing our doubts with honesty and honor, we learn privately and progressively that doubt is not only the darkness of the questioning night; it is the light that comes with the dawn, shining through the mists which prevail."

Any sturdy and resilient Deity is surely unfazed by earthlings voicing doubts about and wrestling with its nature. An evolved God or Goddess welcomes the critical way in religion. As A. Powell Davies stated it:

> *God, being godly, is in no need of defense. What kind of God could be who needed security measures to be protected. For God lives in the open mind, in the power of thought, the voice of truth, the inner impulse of honesty. God needs no protection, no shelter, no defense. Just give God room.*

An intentionally pluralistic religion, Unitarian Universalism invites, nay challenges, us to select the brand of agnosticism most fitting our personal quest. And, as with atheism, there are varieties to be encountered and selected.

George Smith astutely observes that either one can be an "agnostic theist who believes in the existence of god, but maintains that the nature of god is unknowable (the medieval Jewish philosopher, Maimonides, is an example of this position) *or* one can be an agnostic atheist, for whom not only is the *nature* of any supernatural being unknowable, but the *existence* of a supernatural being is unknowable as well." Take your pick.

When Moses sought to know exactly who Yahweh was, so that he could be surer of his religious mission, God replied in cryptic language: "I am who I am," summarily dismissing Moses' quest for certitude. It's not that we just don't know; it's that we cannot know: such is the posture of strong agnosticism.

A further distinction. *Agnostics* don't know, while *ignostics* (a word coined by Rabbi Sherwin Wine, the founder of humanistic Judaism) don't care about God. There appear to be agnostics who dwell secure amidst the state of unknowing and those who covet more edification concerning the Eternal. The former are relatively comfortable, the latter remain fidgety.

It has been posited that atheists and believers are more fanatical than agnostics because they have assumed firmer, if not final, stands. Agnostics seem to be taking the safer, middle-of-the-road position. They resist cockiness. They don't want to make presumptions or take leaps of faith unnecessarily. As author Julia Cameron puts it in her book *God Is Dog Spelled Backwards*: "I'm an agnostic because I'm not arrogant enough to be an atheist."

Yet some have criticized agnostics as being spineless and wishy-washy, while others carp about their seemingly hardened, noncommittal ways. Agnostics have even been caricatured as being unwilling to admit that a rainbow is beautiful or to recognize a divine epiphany when struck in the heart by one.

Scientific theologian John Templeton is patently suspicious of this posture: "The more committed agnostics are to their doubt, the less humble or open-minded they are. Only that doubt which is truly humble, sincerely open-minded, should be labeled agnostic. Only the man or woman who admits the possibility of being wrong is a humble agnostic." But doesn't the same critique obtain for atheists and affirmatists? The sincerity of another seeker can always be thrown into question. We would do well to slacken our criticism of another; for it's beguiling to see the speck in our neighbor's eye and miss the log in our own.

The goal is to remain open-minded—neither closed nor empty but open-minded. Easier said than done. Authentic openness banks on maintaining a sense of humility—one of the least appreciated and under-practiced virtues in human interchange.

The sources section of our Unitarian Universalist Purposes and Principles warns against "idolatries of the mind and spirit." In a lover's quarrel with God, the fundamental attitude of humility alone enables us to counter the allure of idolatry. Humility encourages us to preserve a flexible disposition as we cultivate any relationship with divine mystery, reminding us that our hunches might prove wrong.

True *humanity* is both literally and spiritually related to our being humane, being humorous, and being humble. In the last analysis, humility beckons us to define ourselves in terms of human duties and yearnings. We aren't the center of the universe, no matter how bloated our egos might grow.

We humans are integral contributors, to be sure, even co-partners in the ongoing cosmic flow, but we didn't start creation, our record is checkered at sustaining it, and we won't likely end it. We are midstreamers, earthlings who have come from the dirt—the humus (another root of the word human)—and we shall return to the dirt. That's our story...a noble yet humble one.

And with the sacred interval that's entrusted to each of us, liberal religion urges us never to betray the magnificence of our humanity. It exhorts earthlings to live our days with overflowing humaneness and bellies bursting with humor, and, as Micah phrases it: "to do justice, to love kindness and to walk humbly with our God."

As proper agnostics, Unitarian Universalists don't possess the luxury of freezing our minds or tethering our spirits. We must keep on keeping on, engaged in lifelong questing. For us, revelation is never sealed. As fellow-traveler Jack Mendelsohn presses: "Nothing is settled, everything matters."

One commentator has mused that "of all species of life on Earth, humans are the one that wants to know." We refuse to recline in premature ignorance. Unitarian Universalists may eschew a finalized faith system, but we surely harbor an attitude of faith—cautious but never cynical, equally reverent and reasonable as we engage matters holy.

Simone Weil wrote: "In what concerns divine things, belief is not appropriate. Only certainty will do. Anything less than certainty is unworthy of God." We beg to differ. Freethinkers testify that God is not miffed by our lack of certitude. God is averse to an unchanging or vacant mind but respects the sincere mind…replete with moments of both puzzlement and sharpness.

Unitarian Universalists are content to dwell in mystery without succumbing to either magic or mystification. Creative doubting can furnish a constructive path to uncovering fragments of the Holy. An enjoyable path as well, where one can be "happily agnostic," to use Alan Nordstrom's felicitous phrase.

The term agnostic, from the Greek, *a-gnostos,* translates as "not knowing" and specifically refers to one who says, "I do not know." The Sanskrit antecedent of the Greek contained additional emotional overtones: "to stand in awe before the unknown." Standing in awe means more than merely being ignorant or nonchalant or dumbstruck. It marks active reverence.

One of the world's most prominent theologians, Thomas Aquinas, upon completing 38 treatises, 3000 articles, and 10,000 objections of his *Summa Theologica* (a major intellectual achievement of western civilization) abruptly quit his work in 1273, after a mystical experience while celebrating Mass. Aquinas confided to his secretary that he would write nothing more: "I can do no more, such things have been revealed to me that all I have written seems to me as so much straw…This is what is ultimate in the human knowledge of God—to know that we do not know God." Here was the prince of systematic theologians confessing his deeply felt agnosticism.

Indisputably, one can be a reverent agnostic, singing with the psalmist, "Great is the Lord, and greatly to be praised; his greatness is unsearchable."

There is a time in the religious sojourn to voice our affirmations with clarity and cogency. There is also a season to show the courage of our confusions. And, furthermore, part of the religious quest impels us to surrender to what the Buddhists call *sunyata*: emptiness or void…a reality that plainly cannot be pinned down as this or that. Emptiness is emptiness, the void is void and to be experienced, even celebrated, as such.

The agnostic proudly identifies with sacred journeyers such as the Muslim who speaks of a quaking heart and a stuttering voice in the presence of God; the person in the Christian scriptures who cries out: "Lord, I believe, help my unbelief!"; and St. Anselm of Canterbury, the great theologian of the Middle Ages, who posited *fides quaerens intellectum*…namely, "faith in search of understanding." These spiritual travelers embodied a reverent agnosticism.

Mirroring this same ancestry, Sam Keen, in his incisive volume entitled *Hymns to an Unknown God*, considers his most mature theological position to be one that combines agnosticism with trust:

> *I choose to trust the surrounding mystery out of which I emerged and into which I will disappear in death and to rest secure within the darkness of the unknowable One….I am not uncomfortable in saying that my trust in the ultimate context of my life is invested in God, provided the word "God" is not used more than once a year and is then handled like the Ark of the Covenant.*

Huston Smith, a world religions specialist, has playfully remarked: "A human trying to understand God is like a dog contemplating humans. They know something about the other, but not everything." Yes, such is the plight of the agnostic—sometimes perturbed and perturbing, but more often than not...aglow with sufficient calm. Admitting that we possess but partial knowledge keeps our egos in check and our souls stirring, advancing, pursuing omens and locales of divine portent.

IV. AFFIRMATISM: A DEVOUT YES

May I, composed of eros and dust, beleaguered by the same negation and despair, show an affirming flame.

—W. H. Auden

When you search for me, you will find me; if you seek me with all your heart, I will let you find me, says the Lord.

—Jeremiah 29:12-14

What is meant by affirmatism with respect to the question of God? We make something *firm* by both saying and doing it. Affirm is a stronger term than believe, think, or hope because it invites attachment. The affirmations we venture concerning God must be confirmed in action. As T. S. Eliot says in "Ash Wednesday": "We dare not affirm before the world but deny between the rocks." The only affirmations worthy of the name are those lived in the interstices, between the rocks, of our very existence. All else is abstraction, not affirmation.

Recognizing the gifts of the naysaying and questioning attitudes within Unitarian Universalism, we are also charged to make affirmations. Central to a mature religious sensibility is the capacity to maintain a hopeful (neither pessimistic nor optimistic) attitude toward the Creation. Therefore, the nature of God poses a less crucial question than what our god-cept enables or challenges us to be and do.

As colleague Barbara Merritt proposes:

I believe that our theology can best be perceived in how we prioritize our time, how we forgive and how we stay open and trusting and receptive to help.

Former UUA President William Schulz phrases the issue similarly:

It is a failure of the imagination to believe that the important question about God is whether He or She exists. The important question is: "Is my attitude toward creation one of trust, generosity, and enchantment or suspicion, indifference, and cynicism?"

While the existence of God cannot be conclusively proven, God's importance in our daily lives can often be vividly demonstrated. Hence, the litmus theological test, for our tradition, is: Does believing in a loving God makes us loving? What kind of people do we become when we hold in creative tension the sparring notions of atheism, agnosticism, and affirmatism? Do we, in fact, become a people of critical minds, compassionate hearts, and welcoming hands?

In the midst of healthy noes and perennial maybes, the affirmatist is willing to venture a steady, unyielding Yes to existence in its entirety. Dag Hammarskjold wrote in his personal reflections, *Markings*:

I don't know who—or what—put the question, I don't know when it was put. I don't even remember answering. But at some moment I did answer "Yes" to Someone or something. And from that

hour I was certain that existence is
meaningful and that, therefore, my life, in
self-surrender, had a goal.

The Talmudic tale reminds us that when Moses struck the Dead Sea with his wand, nothing happened, but the sea opened only when the first person plunged in, took the risk, voiced a full-souled *Yes* to Life, Life, Life.

So, when do we experience God? When we say Yes to Life with our entire beings. The affirmatist maintains that Yes is perhaps the central synonym for God. But one huge Yes will not suffice. We must embody affirmatism in the minute exchanges of our daily trek: giving generously of our time, our chutzpah, our resources. I like to think of yea-sayers as explorers, because once we have sought and found smudges of divine fingerprints, we are eager to investigate our discoveries in some depth. Indeed, we seekers become finders become explorers in the ever-evolving religious jaunt.

However, too frequently while waiting for the grand epiphany or the magical moment we miss signs of the Infinite strewn along the path. We must unfasten our eyes and slow our pace to experience the Holy in the commonplace. As Annie Dillard puts it: "Every day is a god, each day is a god, and holiness holds forth in time. I worship each god, I praise each day." Whether eating or sleeping, earning our livelihood or shaping a home, "divine sparks" (the Jewish term) are omnipresent if we are perceptive and receptive. Walt Whitman states it memorably:

Why should I wish to see God better than
this day? I see something of God each

hour of the twenty-four, and each moment then. In the faces of men and women I see God, and in my own face in the glass; I find letters from God dropped in the street, and every one is signed by God's name, and I leave them where they are, for I know that others will punctually come forever and ever.

The fancy name for locating God in the midst of daily traffic is variously phrased "panentheism" or "holistic ecofeminism" and represents an attractive theological alternative for Unitarian Universalists. Panentheism envisions the interdependence of all reality. It attests that the entire Cosmos is shot through with sacredness. God is *in* everything but, unlike, pantheism, is not equatable with or exhausted by the universe. Panentheism retains the Otherness or Transcendence of God.

Most traditional theology has focused upon *definition*, whereas Unitarian Universalists emphasize *location*. Remember, the poet Rainer Maria Rilke spoke about God in terms of a direction rather than an object. It is impossible to define the *who* or *what* of deity, but it proves beneficial to suggest *when* and *where* intimations of God or Goddess may appear. Whereas we cannot find conclusive evidence *for* God, we can experience multiple evidences *of* God. The ensuing section will manifest some of the surprise spots, or what Thoreau called the "lurking-places," where God is sighted in our lives.

Unitarian Universalist affirmatists speak with tentative assurance, not cockiness, recalling that God travels incognito, under pseudonyms, and materializes in unexpected places. There are several inexplicable, eye-popping encounters with God in the Hebrew scriptures.

Remember what happened to Jacob when he reclined in what he took to be a God-forsaken place and suddenly entertained one of the most marvelous visions of the entire Bible: "And Jacob awoke from his sleep and said, 'Surely God was in this place and I, I did not know!'" Yahweh came to Jacob not in the shrine or place of worship but in the midst of a tedious journey and in the prosaic task of setting up camp in the desert. Jacob immediately built an altar right there in a vain attempt to regularize the unpredictable. But it couldn't be done; God refused to be enshrined. Still does.

Theophanies intrude in peculiar places and ways. In most God-sightings—such as those of Amos, Job, and Micaiah—the deity is either not described at all or little content of the vision is reported. When Moses and the elders ascend to the top of the mountain, the narrator describes only what is under God's feet. And bear in mind that Elijah didn't find God in the earthquake or the wind or the fire, the normal ways in his time for bona fide theophanies, but in "a still small voice" or as one translator poetically phrases it, "the sound of a soft stillness."

My point is that the Eternal exhibits in ways beyond human calculation and control, confronting us in startling, even disquieting, fashion sometimes, as when Isaiah announced that God was working through the pagan Assyrians to arouse the Israelites from their disobedience.

We earthlings must rest content with angles and inklings of the Everlasting One. Abraham Heschel used to say that we are more likely to find God's fingerprints on a kitchen table than on a holy altar. "Supernatural splendor emanates from ordinary acts." Sage religiosity is one of awe rather than analysis—freeing one's eyes and heart for radical wonder. Listen to the sentiments of poet Mary Oliver: "When it's over, I want to say: all my life I was a bride married to amazement. I was the bridegroom, taking the world into my arms."

But locating the Holy remains a tricky endeavor. The Jewish tradition properly humbles any and all seekers when it recounts that even Moses himself views but the hind-parts of Yahweh:

> *Then I shall take away my hand and you will see my back-parts, but my face must not be seen.*

—Exodus 33:23

Indeed, the deliverer of the Ten Commandments is not allowed to see Yahweh and live, which means that we can't see the face because God never shows it directly, or it would terrorize or humble us. Worse yet, we might provincialize the vision, then stop growing ourselves, even exclude others. Therefore, Moses shielded himself from divine impact in the crevice of a rock, where he could catch a fleeting glimpse of Yahweh, as he departed, in a kind of hindsight. We humans never get a direct, clean shot of God's face, only moving snapshots of the hindparts. But such will do; they must suffice.

There is more. Yahweh simply likes playing hide-and-seek with us: "Truly, thou art a God who hidest thyself" (Isaiah 45:15). This exclamation of Isaiah is repeated in the cries of the Psalmist and Job. The metaphorical phrase, "God hides His face," occurs over thirty times in the Hebrew Bible. Hence, Yahweh was frequently veiled in the scriptures, even to those who trusted him, so much so that Pascal was moved to assert that no religion that fails to admit the hiddenness of God can be regarded as true.

Customarily, we associate "the hiddenness of God" with inaccessibility or a sense of foreboding. To be sure, the Great Spirit is inscrutable, but couldn't it also be that God's evasiveness serves Her/His/Its own longing for relationship?

Meister Eckhart expressed divine mystery well when he said that "God is like a person who clears his throat while hiding and so gives himself away." So, there is high joy for God in being discovered, however partially, by us humans. The *deus absconditus* is also the *deus ludens*, a God disclosed in fun and tomfoolery. Just like when we play hide-and-go-seek as children, we want to hide but also to be found. God does this, children follow suit, and we adults would remember the fun as well.

In any case, affirmatists recognize that we always live in relationship with an absent presence, a God who withdraws and advances, conceals and reveals. Such is the paradox of questing after God. To complicate matters, when Isaiah or Paul is having a vision of God, others around them rarely are partaking of it. Humans simply never share the same epiphanies or mystical moments—the best we can manage is exchanging notes in open company. Therefore, we need the critique and challenge of a beloved community lest our revelations become privatistic or unbending.

One more thought. God hides, but so do we. That's what the Garden Story is all about. We commit a wrong, grow ashamed, then hide ourselves from the presence of God among the trees of the garden. God seeks us, calling out: "Where are you?"—a question more to do with morality than geography. God shows us Its back and moves on. We turn our backs as well. The question remains: Will we stay in hiding or meet the Creative One halfway? In emerging from self-imposed hiddenness, we may enter the presence of a living God. At least, there's always that possibility.

An anecdote told of Henry David Thoreau, as a young child, augurs early panentheistic inclinations:

> *When his mother found Henry still awake in bed she asked, "Why, Henry dear, why don't you go to sleep?" "Mother," said he, "I have been looking through the stars to see if I couldn't see God behind them."*

The rest of his life Thoreau searched for and found the divine "through the stars," embedded, as it were, in the flow of the natural domain.

Panentheism holds that the Creator is discernible in but not exhausted by the plants, animals, humans of creation. It makes room for the mystery of soul, the unfathomableness of nature, the wholly "otherness" of God.

I remember leading a children's worship service years back. Kindergarten through sixth-grade children were gathered in a beautiful chapel setting. We were conversing about God, a ticklish theological term for adults, less intimidating for guileless kids.

One of the older children, a bright sixth grader, rose to her feet and with great self-assurance, uttered: "I think that God is a force!" She spoke with such imperiousness that discussion promptly ceased. The little ones in the room gazed up at the sixth grader in adulation, as if to concede that God's nature had just been definitively revealed. Only adults and God itself could be larger, in their eyes, than this budding teenager.

Then one of our irrepressible five-year olds broke the silence and blurted out, "Hey, I saw a forest once!"

Then, with a big smile on my face, and even greater one in my heart, I reached out to appreciate the gifts of the big child and the little one and all sizes in between gathered in our Chapel that morning. And these words tumbled forth from my throat: "Yes, children, God is a *force* who can be found in the *forest* and oh, so many other neat and wild places as well."

With this paradigm in mind, we now set out for some unforeseen, perhaps even startling, "lurking-places" of the divine. I forewarn us to travel equipped with keen vision and unrestrained heart.

V. SIX LURKING-PLACES OF GOD

*My profession is to be always on the alert to find
God in nature, to know his lurking-places, to attend
all the oratorios, the opera, in nature.*

—Henry David Thoreau

*God does not speak prose, but communicates with
us by hints, omens, inferences and dark
resemblances in objects around us.*

—Ralph Waldo Emerson

When focusing on where to look for God in the crazy tangle of the cosmic web, it's seductive to fixate on familiar haunts, such as natural beauty, sexual communion, musical epiphanies, truth-speaking, and deeds of goodness. While conceding the richness of well-trod avenues to Divine Presence, the challenge of Unitarian Universalist affirmatism remains to stalk the Holy in fresh hangouts.

Two of our most prominent 20th-century Unitarian Universalist theologians, Charles Hartshorne and Henry Nelson Wieman, were proclaimers of this serendipitous view of the divine. Hartshorne, who maintained a vigorous mind to the end of his 103 years, was influenced deeply by both his father, a practicing theologian, and his mother, who inspired him with a simple statement that he never forgot. "Charles," she told him when he was a boy, "life is big, life is big." Consequently, Hartshorne always expounded a theology that was expansive in scope and vast in spirit.

Hartshorne concluded that God breaks into human experience through the truly novel and creative. Wieman developed a philosophy of naturalistic theism where God is understood to be a power inherent in the universe that "persuades" or "lures" all living things forward toward their ultimate fulfillment. He named that power "Creative Interchange"—the universal force that, when enjoined, utterly changes us. Therefore, to participate in the radically open, interdependent, transformative venture called Unitarian Universalism meant linking in faithful partnership with Creativity.

What follows are but sample lurking-places where Unitarian Universalists might greet some portion—front or back or side—of the Eternal Spirit. A handful of six modest and unanticipated locales where traces of the divine arrive both as welcome guest and unsettling intruder.

You are certainly nudged to offer your own additions and corrections to my theological minutes. Unitarian Universalists unqualifiedly adhere to Buddha's admonition "to be a lamp unto yourself." But one prudent note: please don't quibble unduly with my choices. I invite you, instead, to be aroused, even a bit unnerved, by them. My notions are meant to be evocative, not definitive—a commentary geared to stir your own hunt for a flock of original god-sightings.

One more word of caution. Jewish mystics suggest that the whole Torah is but one long name of God. Scrolls display words running into each other. This signifies that holiness is unified, and, furthermore, that it is well-nigh impossible to disentangle the sundry sightings of the divine, let alone spot them all. So, open your hands, unclench your mind, and relax your entire being. Wonders await!

SERVICE

The act is love and God is love. And when we love,
we god.

—Carter Heyward

Find God by becoming a partner with God in
healing, repairing and transforming the world.
Don't look for God, but become Her ally and She
will find you.

—Michael Lerner

A prime, yet oft-ignored, lurking-place for the divine is manifest through service. The mystical activist Gandhi was clear that God came to him not through science, reason, or intuition so much as through action. Encountering God for Unitarian Universalists, as well, is ultimately less an issue of thinking the right thoughts so much as doing the right things. One's espoused theology pales beside one's practiced faith. Our way of religion strives to major in results not rhetoric.

In the Christian scriptures, Jesus clearly repudiates the pious who go about boasting: "Lord, Lord!," then fail to follow his teachings. The Bible, from front to back, is far more interested in deeds of goodness than creeds about God. Elie Wiesel alerted: "God is telling us: 'I can take care of my own ideas, images, theories— you take care of my creation!'" Our mission is to be concerned about earthly service not heavenly speculation, to be riveted on economic justice not metaphysics.

Carter Heyward claims that we are involved in "godding or doing god" whenever we make justice and share joy with the whole creation. The Beatitudes accent this same linkage when Jesus says: "Blessed are the merciful for they shall see God." This means that signs of the Holy appear in the countenance of those we serve and love.

Rachel Naomi Remen, a medical pioneer in the mind-body health movement and author of *Kitchen Table Wisdom*, differentiates service from fixing or helping. She writes:

> *Fixing is a form of judgment that denotes inequality of expertise that can easily become a moral distance. When helping we also imply that someone is needier than we are. A hierarchy is constructed. Conversely, we cannot serve at a distance. We can only serve that to which we are profoundly connected, that which we are willing to touch. We serve life not because it is broken but because it is holy.*

Thus, anytime we are in service to another, to our community, or to the Earth, we are doing the work of God. We are God's hands.

There is a beautiful expression in the Gospels that appears twelve times and is used exclusively in reference to Jesus or God. That expression is "to be moved with compassion." The Greek verb *splangchnizomai* reveals to us the deep and powerful meaning of this term. The *splangchna* are the entrails of the body, or as we might say today, the guts. They are the place where our most intimate and intense emotions are located—the passional center of our rejoicing, our anguishing, our raging, our serving instincts.

Jesus was no formal theologian but a practical one. The Nazarene possessed no systematic doctrine of God, mentioning God only rarely. Nevertheless, Jesus aspired to incarnate what he knew of ultimacy and goodness. He *godded*, to use Heyward's astute phrase. Or as Abraham Heschel states it: "God is hiding in the world and our task is to let the divine emerge from our deeds." Therefore, as we earthlings exude compassion, we ourselves share in divinity.

Unitarian Universalists are parodied by the orthodox for "being thick on ethics and thin on theology," yet, in truth, we belong to that tribe of religious explorers who, like Jesus, were loving servants more than ardent scholars. Our theology is incarnated through our ethics. What follows are some elements of a theology of service or compassion.

First, we believe in serving, not saving (that's God's work), those members of humanity hurting in our very midst, not just people in faraway places. Recall the judgment day parable when Jesus pointedly says that if we have been serving the least of our sisters and brothers, we have been serving him. That is, if we truly have been clothing the naked, visiting prisoners, taking care of the wounded, the hungry, the homeless, the sick, then we have been displaying compassion not only to these folks but to the Nazarene as well.

Second, Unitarian Universalists hold that there are no ulterior motives in caring for one's sister or brother. Compassion is never to be used as a warm-up or softener for religious conversion. Service isn't a means to some end; it *is* the end.

Countless religions that have done marvelous work with the poor still demand the hearing of sermons before the offering of food or shelter. Our way differs. We believe that religion is served whenever food is served and shelter is provided. In the very act of compassion, our faith is made visible. Whenever humans love, God abides.

Third, as "freethinking mystics with hands," we want to be realistic as well as idealistic in our experiments with compassion. It's easy to become quickly frustrated, then angry, even resentful, in working with marginalized people. We want them to change, and not only change, but to end up looking and acting pretty much like ourselves.

Well, the "highest possible functioning" for countless desperate and depressed people will seldom match standards of social "normality." That isn't their goal, and it shouldn't be ours for them either. The job of compassion is nothing more and nothing less than enabling those in need to live decently and with sufficient dignity.

Fourth, our theology of service demands cooperation rather than lone-rangerism. This seems self-evident in addressing long-term, economic-moral struggles. But authentic teamwork is difficult to achieve in our insulated, egotistical culture. Nonetheless, the truth remains: if we are bound together in causing the conditions that produce poverty and bigotry, we must unite hearts and hands in combating these conditions.

We must serve across faith traditions, as well as bridge the public and private sectors of our world. We must stop agonizing and start organizing. We must cease bickering and begin cooperating.

Finally, our approach to compassion would heed the biblical admonition: "and if anyone forces you to go one mile, go with that person two miles" (Matthew 5: 41-42). The first mile Jesus is talking about refers to compassion as direct service. The second mile delves behind the presenting ache and lifts up a human being starved for affection and meaning.

The second mile includes situational counseling, employment and housing assistance, legislative advocacy. The second mile goes beyond today and beyond even a particular client and works to alter the inhumane and unjust conditions of our society that create socio-economic-racial devastation in the first place.

Written on the walls of a Spanish harbor is the aphorism: "I am seeking God, but I do not find God. I am seeking myself but I do not find me. But I do find my neighbor and the three of us get on our way together."

In every religion, a sincere, merciful exchange with the stranger is the highest expression of faith, and, in fact, the Divine frequently comes cloaked in the guise of the outcast, the fool, the guest. "Hospitality to strangers is greater than reverence for the name of God" declares the Hebrew proverb.

The ritual bond of host and guest demonstrates our common humanity. If we fail to be responsive guests and hosts, we will never experience the full meaning of being either human or religious. Ancient hosts were required to regard a guest as one who might be as likely powerful as helpless, might prove to be a blessing or a burden. Each guest could be anyone: a king, a murderer in flight, a returning daughter, a god or goddess.

Yet the Great Spirit doesn't only appear in the guise of the downtrodden or foreigner. It also enters our reality whenever we look at children with an active gaze and level glance, resolve estrangement with a lover or colleague, or, perhaps most challengingly, through affirming the very enemy with whom our destiny and survival are intertwined. Remember, God is full of surprises, both pleasant and disquieting ones.

The core of our enduring Universalist gospel is God's unconditional regard for life. Whereas we humans can never *repay* this boundless love, we can and must *return* the favor. Loved, we love in reply: through active, direct service, by being carriers of compassion to Earth and its inhabitants.

Our early Universalist forebears spent occasional moments chatting about God and the New Jerusalem, but their chief concern was focused on the earthly life. They felt that a more heavenly existence could be delivered upon this known, precious globe. So, Universalists attacked the prevailing belief in eternal damnation while focusing on serving their sisters and brothers during this lifetime. All social improvement— be it penal reform or humane treatment of criminals, animals, and children—issued from their gratitude for gifts of a loving God.

Unitarian theologian Wallace Robbins echoed the same sentiment:

> *Ours is a faith of moral work not because we think morality is a sufficient religion but because we know of no better way of showing our gratitude to God, and our confidence in one another.*

STUFF

It is not a distant, mysterious God to whom we make appeal or even the cold vagaries of Progress, Evolution, Creativity, or History. The gods and goddesses—or, if you prefer, the most precious and profound—are accessible to us in the taste of honey and the touch of stone. And this in turn is why we Unitarian Universalists love the earth, honor the human body, and bless the stars. Religion is not just a matter of Things Unseen. For us the Holy is not hidden but is displayed in the real workings of the world.

—William Schulz

Now it is time that gods came walking out of lived-in Things.

—Rainer Maria Rilke

What is there of the divine in a load of bricks? What is there of the divine in a barber's shop? Much. All.

—Ralph Waldo Emerson

Blessed be you, universal matter, unmeasurable time, boundless ether, triple abyss of stars and atoms and generations; you who by overflowing and dissolving our narrow standards of measurement reveal to us the dimensions of God.

—Teilhard de Chardin

The whole world is full of God.

—Isaiah 6:3

While sleuthing out lurking-places for the divine in the world, one must scour the continuum of holiness—from humans to animals, from plants to rocks to material objects. Indeed, medical doctor and scientist James Lovelock writes:

> *There is no clear distinction anywhere on the Earth's surface between living and nonliving matter. There is merely a hierarchy of intensity going from the "material" environment of the rocks and the atmosphere to the living cells.*

Everything is alive, surging, restless, and possesses animus. Being immersed in the mundane *stuff* of the evolving ecosystem we experience various signatures of God.

Naturalists immediately greet animals and plants as an extension of God's body or as spiritual guides dwelling in our midst. One only has to read the exquisite writings of 19th-century Unitarian transcendentalists as well as contemporary naturalists like Lewis Thomas and Annie Dillard to discern their unabashed religious tone and substance. Diane Ackerman portrays her mystical sensibility as follows:

> *There are different terms I suppose you could apply to my brand of spirituality. You might call it ecospirituality. I think of myself as an earth ecstatic.*

Our religious forebear Henry David Thoreau put it similarly: "We live but a fraction of our life. Why do we not let on the flood, raise the gates, and set all our wheels in motion? Those who have ears let them hear.

Employ your senses." Thoreau was not a sensually indulgent person deficient in moral pursuits, excessively fleshy. Hardly. For Thoreau, employing ones senses was a critical spiritual discipline. In experiencing nature up close, Thoreau felt that he was encountering the holy, the transcendent, God directly—body to body, so to speak.

Mystical naturalism holds a hallowed spot in our history. Even the ardent humanists in our fold often refer to numinous truth garnered while encountering the wonders of the cosmos. And whereas the signers of the original (1933) Humanist Manifesto were not supernaturalists, they were naturalists. Listen to the refrain of founder E. Burdette Backus: "We humans are co-partners with great Nature who has produced us...." His humanism, while emphasizing human purposes and fulfillment, was always responsive to the presence of transcendent creativity at work in the natural order. In truth, whether cosmologists are believers or not, they are uniformly swayed by the sweep and majesty of this extraordinary universe.

Animals as well as plants embody the tracks of godness amidst the stuff of the cosmos. Let me briefly reference the divinity of our four-legged kin.

Animals, like humans, are creatures with an inherent worth and dignity, and must be reverenced precisely because they cannot speak for themselves. Unitarian Universalist minister, Gary Kowalski, puts it compellingly in his trenchant volume entitled *The Souls of Animals*:

> *Animals are not our property or chattel,*
> *but our peers and fellow travelers. Like*

us, they have their own likes and dislikes, fears and fixations. They have plans and purposes as important to them as ours are to us. Animals not only have biologies, they also have biographies. We can appreciate the lives of animals but not appropriate them. For they have their own lives to lead. When we treat them as if they were mere biological machines, we injure both their nature and our own. They are our spiritual colleagues and emotional companions. We know this to be true less through debate than through direct experience.

Just as God appears to us as we serve our neighbors, so also God is disclosed in our lives as we respectfully companion critters. Naturally, not all animals are social or altruistic, but neither are humans. Both species do destructive things.

Furthermore, there are disasters, both natural and inexplicable at the heart of this awesome universe. The Creation is clearly not an unabashed reservoir of wonder and delight. Yet many are the process theologians in our Unitarian Universalist camp who hold that whereas God is not omnipotent or causally in charge, the Eternal Spirit moves in the throes of natural and human evil trying to bring respite and healing. God is a power that influences but does not control reality.

But when exactly is God present and when absent, when visibly active and when detached? It's hard to know. As comedian Rodney Dangerfield smirked: "I put a seashell to my ear and got a busy signal." A posture of agnosticism is about as far as my mind extends on these matters.

However, if the Creator is celebrated throughout the Creation, we must take into account the entirety of existence. As Unitarian Universalists we revere the whole cosmos, from soil to sky to stone. We maintain that all existence radiates a divine glow. We resonate with the wisdom of the Hasidic master who once said:

> *When you walk across the fields with your mind pure and holy, then from all the stones, and all growing things, and all animals, the sparks of their soul come out and cling to you, and then they are purified and become a holy fire in you.*

Speaking of stones, Carolyn and I were drawn to southern Africa in 1995, because we had been captivated by the exquisite sculpture of the Shona tribe of Zimbabwe, when we attended a show at the Natural History Museum in Balboa Park in our hometown of San Diego.

Shona sculpture is embedded in the mystical folk culture of the Shona people and emanates from the deep recesses of their creative soul. Now, of all the materials available for carving, stone is the most difficult. Shona craftspeople specifically utilize the naked coarseness of natural elements to express their purest creativity. The faith of the Shona people is intensely animistic, and they affirm the spirituality of divinized matter.

However, we must retreat in history. Shona sculpture has come into worldwide prominence only in the last few decades, although the innate skill of the craftspeople is evident in what remains of the magnificent Great Zimbabwe wall, the largest ancient structure in sub-Saharan Africa, which served as a temporal and religious capital in the Middle Ages.

It took thousands of hands to hew out millions of granite blocks for the elliptical Great Enclosure alone. Despite 100 years of systematic effort by imperialist governments to ascribe the origins of Great Zimbabwe to someone else—anyone other than the indigenous African people—conclusive proof of its Shona origins was already in place in 1932 after a British archaeologist verified it. Even up to independence in 1980, the Rhodesian government ignored the evidence and continued to support far-fetched fantasies of foreign influence and habitation. That tragic story is illustrative of the devastation wrought by colonial oppression.

The Shona sculptures are rightly named "spirits in stone," and they capture earth's kaleidoscopic array of stuff in their creative art, ranging from humans to animals to plain objects of natural beauty. A holy spirit permeates all of existence for the Shona people, animate and inanimate alike.

A couple of examples of the sacred suffusing the animal realm. *Mvuu* or the Hippo, represents the spirit of shyness. As Shona legend has it, the hippo begged God to allow it to remain in the water all day long to hide its perceived ugliness. The tale continues that God made a covenant with the hippo: "Okay, mvuu, yours is an honest and honorable plea. You can bask in the water to your heart's desire, as long as you promise never to eat my fish!" So a hallowed bargain was struck, and to this day the hippopotamus remains a vegetarian and is the symbol of keeping one's word to God and all others as well.

Then there's *Dacha*, the magical frog. To the Shona, the frog possesses mystical charm. The spirits of one's ancestors, wanting to protect the dreams of the children, called upon the timid, tiny frog to croon her bold joyous songs only at night.

The ancestors felt that this would frighten evil demons away from insidiously entering the children's dreams and causing harm. The modest frog said she would sing in exchange for being respected by both humans and deities—despite being so small and seemingly insignificant. So, to this day, the Shona natives send forth a holy greeting of gratitude to the frog for her intrepid singing that protects their beloved children at night.

Finally, in addition to the remarkable Great Zimbabwe stone ruins and the exquisite Shona stone sculpture, Zimbabwe possesses the biggest concentration of rock art in the world, finely realized paintings of animals and people in everyday life. The very word Zimbabwe derives from the Shona term for "venerated houses of stone."

We moderns still say "solid as a rock" or "its foundation is set on stone." However, as naturalistic essayist Scott Sanders points out: "Rocks are not fixed. Waters carve them, winds abrade them, heat and cold fracture them." And in the case of the Shona tribe, people boldly shape them.

Beauty floods our lives via ordinary things, inorganic objects as well. Unitarian author Charles Dickens was widely praised for "his deep reverence for the household gods," which meant that Dickens eyed the marvelous in the mundanities of his everyday life. This appreciation of stuff reminds one of a rudimentary poem in Marge Piercy's collection entitled *My Mother's Body*, where she lists and explicates the following "Six Underrated

Pleasures:" folding sheets, picking pole beans, taking a hot bath, sleeping with cats, planting bulbs, and canning. Each of us could deftly generate our own comparable list of physical delights.

Empty the pockets of any five-year-old child and you possess a mirror of the thought world of that child. I would add: look at what things we teenagers and adults store in our closets or save in our wallets, and the contents of our convictions are divulged. As Unitarian Universalist religious educator Edith Hunter regularly reminded: "Perhaps we should realize that our need is not to find something to believe but rather to discover what our lives indicate that we believe right now."

When I was living alone for a month in the Temeculan woods north of San Diego in 1990, I grew an affection for the lifeless treasures that filled my small cabin. I spent time engrossed in contemplation of the commonplace, in viewing and being stared back at by inert things such as my reliable, green Coleman lantern, a yellow-coated vegetable pot, the one and only stubby glass, the eccentric floor-length mirror in the bedroom. Meditating upon this stuff would bring me moments of sacred connection with Otherness, a glimpse into the holy amidst the ordinary.

The Zen teacher Soen-Roshi has always made a little bow of gratitude to the world around him. A bow is a wonderful way to appreciate this very moment and pay respectful attention to the world around us. Spirit and enlightenment have everything to do with our being fully present amidst the stuff of this single, precious world— grateful right where we dwell. Bowing fully to each fleeting experience.

Children do not study shoe boxes to manufacture better boxes. They study them because they are. It remains important and necessary to study things for some purpose, but it is *holy* to study them for no purpose. Each item is priceless not because of what it can be used for, but simply because it is.

Being a relatively recent and active grandfather certainly brings home to me this sensitivity to the holy-in-the-ordinary-old . It is seldom the bought toys that galvanize our five-yearTrevor's enthusiasm, but down-to-earth, physical, and quite creaturely little things.

Stuff like the found object on our walks, the scratch on his arm, the rock on the sidewalk that waits to be picked up or kicked, the bird sitting on a telephone wire, the helicopter motoring overhead, or Carolyn's chapstick, which he mentions upon arrival at our house on Wednesdays. Or my guitar pick, around which we play interminably fascinating hide-and-go-seek games. Trevor drops it in the belly of the guitar, and I shake the instrument wildly about until we get it to come out. Then we repeat the game until one of us tires (guess who?), and I place the guitar pick in my coin purse, reminding Trevor that even the pick needs, now and again, to take a nap just like he does.

Carolyn asked the other day why it took our three-year-old granddaughter, Corinne, and me so long to walk the half-a-block to the mailbox to mail letters. "Where were you guys, anyway?" she inquired. "Carolyn, you and I both know what took us so long!" I retorted. We both smiled.

Vincent Van Gogh remarked that "the best way to know God is to love many things." Note he didn't say to love many people or projects or landscapes. No, he said: "to love many things." And Anne Sexton in her poem "Welcome Morning" sings the praises of God being present in the eggs, the kettle, the spoon, the chair, the table of her morning rituals. She writes: "All this is God, right here in my pea-green house each morning...so while I think of it, let me paint a thank-you on my palm for this God, this laughter of the morning, lest it go unspoken. The Joy that isn't shared, I've heard, dies young."

I would bet that each of us has a sacred corner in our home or office or simply in our mind's eye. In our daily life there most likely exists some sort of altar composed of artifacts carrying personal meaning and furnishing us with a window into the divine.

The holiest of my relics hangs around my neck. It depicts the "Tree of Life" enmeshed in a yin-yang universe with branches reaching out in compassion and aspiration and roots going deep into life's humus. It's a modest yet compelling bronze object sculpted by my brother-in-law that I have worn every day of our 28-year-old marriage. It reminds me not only of my love for my wife, Carolyn, but also of my place in this universe as a sacred tree myself—grounded in the soil, generative of trunk, extending my branches in love, sometimes full of leaves, other times barren, always soaring skyward.

One warning: it's tempting to venerate tangible stuff, therewith worshipping golden calves as did the Israelites of yore. But things are merely carriers of divinity—not the Eternal per se.

SILLINESS

I don't say that God is one grand laugh, but I say that you've got to laugh hard before you can get anywhere near God.

—Henry Miller

God plays when he makes the world. I have very little patience with people who rattle on about the Divine Plan ...If God can be said to have a plan at all, it is probably much more like improvisational drama than like the drill-team exercises such people imagine. The highest form of play is precisely turning ourselves on in order to turn others on, it is the offering up of goodness in delight, for delight...

—Robert Capon

In religion, too often the growl of horror takes the place of the howl of laughter. It has generally been the assumption that spirituality and humor are awkward bedfellows. This apparent incompatibility is rooted in early church theologians such as St. Chrysostom, who said: "Laughter does not seem to be a sin, but it leads to sin."

Before the missionaries came, the natives were noted for their full-bodied laughter. But unrestrained tittering seemed "pagan" to the colonizers. After reeducation in Christian ways, indigenous peoples developed a nervous, suppressed laughter known as the "mission giggle."

On the contrary, humor assaults sin. Merry-making brings the Transcendent nigh. We exist to make a joyful noise unto the Lord. Nothing sabotages religion more swiftly than a band of humorless crusaders. Rowing toward God is a serious but not stern business. Foolishness and revelry are necessary to a satisfying trek.

In German the world for blessedness is *saelisch*, which is etymologically related to our English word "silly," reminding sedate types that to be blessed we would do well to become irrepressible practitioners of zaniness. Additionally, the word "enthusiasm" means "God-filled," so as we demonstrate exuberance and joy, our lives emit divinity.

In the spirit of silliness, one is reminded of how Thich Nhat Hanh, the renowned Zen Buddhist monk and peace activist, was lightheartedly depicted by a colleague as "A cross between a cloud, a snail, and a piece of heavy machinery—in short, a true religious presence."

In our American culture we are often on *display*, performing for an audience, or engrossed in *replay*, endlessly digging into our dysfunctional pasts, but we rarely engage in old-fashioned, uninhibited *play*: frolicking with no high purpose in mind, just playing for the sake of playing.

I like what Unitarian Universalist writer Kurt Vonnegut says along this line in his book *Fates Worse than Death*:

> *To all my friends and relatives in Alcoholics Anonymous, I say that they are right to become intoxicated. Life without moments of intoxication is not worth a pitcher of spit, as the felicitous saying goes. They simply chose what was for them a deadly poison on which to get drunk. Good examples of harmless toots are some of the things children do. They get smashed for hours on some strictly*

limited aspect of the Great Big Everything, the Universe, such as water or snow or mud or colors or rocks or echoes or funny sounds from the voiceboxes of banging on a drum and so on. Only two people are involved: the child and the Universe. The child does a little something to the Universe, and the Great Big Everything does something funny or beautiful or something disappointing or scary or even painful in return. The child teaches the Universe how to be a good playmate, to be nice instead of mean.

May we Unitarian Universalists hold our gods and goddesses buoyantly—with a light heart and a light touch—for God is a playful being. The Great Spirit possibly created the world out of boredom, being in dire need of playmates. Through games and song and dance we are ongoingly surprised by evidences of the Sacred breaking into our oft-bleak lives and calling us to amusement. God is definitely about surprise and serendipity and silliness and calls us to follow suit.

The Sufi poet Hafiz remarks: "What is laughter? It is God waking up!" Life is riddled with intractable paradoxes that must be ridden all the way home, and the ride, to be endurable, begs for abundant fun. Are we ready to join God in mutual laughter, in waking up?

Humor is the kindly contemplation of life's incongruities; so is religion. Thus, humor and religion are as Siamese twins; when you tear them asunder, both may wither and die. Residing in the comic mode enables us to laugh at life's folly and flaws while still battling its injustices. Humor is our best antidote to the idolatry that can subtlely infect our atheism, our agnosticism, and our affirmatism.

The *Ramayana* notes that "there are three things that are real: God, human folly, and laughter. The first two are beyond comprehension, so we must do what we can with the third." In fact, it's via laughter that we are able to make connections with God and place human folly in the proper light.

Theology, however insightful and stirring, must never claim too much for itself. Words about God are not God. Language furnishes but pointers, faint echoes of the real thing. Commenting on all the fuss that had been made about his monumental *Church Dogmatics*, Karl Barth, one of the premier Protestant theologians of the 20th century, willingly poked fun at himself:

> *The angels laugh at old Karl. They laugh at him because he tries to grasp the truth about God in a book of Dogmatics. Volume follows volume and each is thicker than the previous one. As they laugh, they say to one another, "Look, here he comes now with his little pushcart full of volumes of the Dogmatics." Truly, the angels laugh.*

In chortling with Barth and at ourselves, we draw closer into the realm of the Creative Spirit. Rigid atheists, lazy agnostics, and smug affirmatists—all find themselves rowing away from the Holy. Only when religion has honored both its serious and funny bones will it settle safe in human hands.

The notable Danish theologian Soren Kierkegaard went to the nubbins of the theological quest when he wrote: "When I was young, I forgot to laugh; later when I opened my eyes and saw reality...I began to laugh and haven't stopped since." May we keep on laughing all the way to our graves and beyond, where we just might join a chorus of chucklers surrounding the Almighty.

We make a joyful noise through singing and dancing as well as play and humor. King David, despite his prodigious wisdom, never tried to prove God; he simply sang the Creator's praises. Tagore says: "God respects us when we talk, but loves us when we sing." Song and dance are embodied theology, what one clergyperson considered, "a body of practical divinity." Indeed.

Few of us in our theologizing will ever become "whirling dervishes," that stately order of Sufi dancers, but when we move our arms and legs in swaying fashion, we are gamboling to the euphony of the Creation. A dervish was asked why he worshipped God through dance. "Because," he replied, "to worship God means to die to self: dancing kills the self. When the self dies, all problems die with it. Where the self is not, Love is, God is."

We are creative beings made in the image of a re-creative Being.

I close this section with some humor that good-naturedly jabs at each of the triple A's—atheism, agnosticism, and affirmatism:

> —On his deathbed, the atheist panicked, looked up to Heaven and pleaded: "Oh, God, if there is a God, save my soul, if I have one."

Excerpts from the homework assignment of Danny Dutton, age 8, from Chula Vista, California in his attempts to explain God:

—One of God's main jobs is making people. He makes them to replace the ones that die so there will be enough people to take care of things on earth. God doesn't make grown-ups, only babies. I think because they are smaller and easier to make. That way, God doesn't have to take up his valuable time teaching them to walk and talk.

—Atheists are people who don't believe in God. I don't think there are any in Chula Vista. At least there aren't any who come to our church.

(Now, whereas that may be the case for Danny's church, it certainly doesn't hold true for our Unitarian Universalist congregations in the same San Diego area.)

—Did you hear about the Unitarian Universalist who married a Jehovah's Witness? Their children still knock on people's doors, but they don't know why.

—A diagnostic is someone who doesn't know whether or not there are two gods.

—I am an agnostic pagan. I doubt the existence of many gods.

—To you I may be an atheist. To God, I'm the Loyal Opposition.

—What does an agnostic dyslexic insomniac think about at night: "I wonder if there really is a dog?"

STRUGGLE

Always God has been struggling, failing and beginning again, falling and rising again. A million times God has been halted, turned aside, defeated. But always, by virtue of the essential divinity that makes God, he has resumed his work. So God has wrestled with the world and is still wrestling. God and the world have evolved together, and are still evolving in a mutual process of creation....This finite God who struggles as we struggle, suffers as we suffer, and who knows not only power and victory but defeat and disappointment, and much weariness, is a being like unto ourselves. He can help us and we can help him. His purpose must be fulfilled through us.

—John Haynes Holmes

We have heard that God is all the goodness, all the sweetness and light and joy in the morning. God may be the chaos, missed in our neatness and order, who shuns the glistening temple to walk in the gray repositories of twisted and divided souls. To see such a God is to seek discomfort, to walk in another's broken shoes through the eye of an inner storm and be bent and twisted with them.

—Edward Frost

Contrary to popular opinion and New Age preoccupation with prosperity and bliss, God moves repeatedly amidst clamor and travail. Historically, seekers have met the Infinite One in bushes that burned, dens of lions and thieves, valleys of shadows. The prophet was correct: "God is like a refiner's fire," where dross and gold are being separated. Wherever there is disquiet, God lurks, habitually stirring things up.

In his recent book, *God at the Edge: Searching for the Divine in Uncomfortable and Unexpected Places*, young Rabbi Niles Elliott Goldstein tells of finding God in scary situations like dog-sledding above the Arctic Circle, being chased by a grizzly bear, and spending the night in a New York City jail. He juxtaposes his own raw experiences and skirmishes with inner demons alongside the testimonies of historical religious figures ranging from St. John of the Cross to Moses Maimonides. As Goldstein puts it:

> *Nietzsche warns us: 'If you gaze long into an abyss, the abyss will gaze back into you.' But there can be darkness without doom. The edge does not have to lead to nihilism. If we are careful, it is possible to recognize, accept, even grow from spirituality's borderlands without being consumed by them.*

Late in his life, psychoanalyst Carl Jung reflected: "To this day, God is the name by which I designate all things which cross my path violently and recklessly, all things which upset my subjective views, plans and intentions and change the course of my life for better or worse." That's pretty strong language, but not an unfamiliar occurrence for wayfarers in our household of faith.

In addition, we don't anticipate final resolution of life's incessant skirmish. Rather we expect to die in midstream, ensconced in a protracted struggle, still rowing toward God.

The story of Jacob wrestling with a being greater than himself in the Hebrew scriptures stands as a paradigm for disclosure of the divine in the throes of strife. After a night of unrelenting scuffle, Jacob exits with a limp and a new name, Israel: "the one who strives or struggles with God."

Israel, throughout its spiritual evolution as a nation, comes to represent a kinfolk willing to rage and grapple openly with God. "Argue with heaven," as the Jewish phrase goes. Cloying or groveling are considered undignified human activities in the whole of Judaic lore. Existential struggle is integral not peripheral to the Jewish quest. Indeed, robust religion has always agreed with Unitarian Carl Sandburg, who imagined that "God grows tired of too many hallelujahs!"

William Butler Yeats, in his poem, *The Four Ages of Man*, addresses what he views as the ultimate task of winter—yielding to God:

> *He with body waged a fight,*
> *But body won; it walks upright.*
> *Then he struggled with the heart;*
> *Innocence and peace depart.*
> *Then he struggled with the mind;*
> *His proud heart he left behind.*
> *Now his wars on God begin;*
> *At stroke of midnight God shall win.*

I personally don't subscribe to such triumphalist language, but Yeats' point holds. We grow through wrestling with God, and not solely at the close of our earthly sojourn, but all along the way. We mature spiritually, as Rilke claims, "by being defeated, decisively, by constantly greater things."

Our lives remain an eternal clash between good and evil, tussling to overcome our baser instincts with measured compassion. We struggle to be responsible citizens and kindly children of the universe. We never cease struggling. And neither does God. Nikos Kazantzakis, a literary philosopher who blended both Christianity and Buddhism in his faith journey, wrote:

> *The search itself—upward and with coherence—perhaps this is the purpose of the Universe. God is the supreme expression of the unwearied and struggling human. Oh, undaunted, unhealable Searcher! The essence of our God is struggle. Pain, joy, and hope unfold and labor within this struggle, world without end.*

Unitarian Universalists resonate with this poetic description of humanity and divinity. At bedrock, we are a movement—ever in motion, often commotion. Consequently, our spiritual forebear David Rhys Williams in his fine book, *Faith Beyond Humanism,* wrote in 1963:

> *God is a struggling Deity—starting with things as they are and endeavoring to bring order out of chaos; to change evil into the good, the good into the better, and the better into the best. God is an experimenting Deity—constantly trying one method and then another to effect ever higher ends, learning from past failures and building on past achievements.*

Yes, our liberating religious heritage has often held that God is a struggling, failing being, who keeps starting over and rising again. A similar scenario to how we human pilgrims navigate the harsh, turbulent waters of existence.

So, we humans are not only evolving, the Supreme Being is also in process. As a co-struggler, God circulates in the midst of sorrow and evil. Elie Wiesel tells the story of a Jew who used to be taunted by his Nazi guards. One day he was ordered to clean out the filthy toilets. A guard standing over him gloatingly shouted out: "Okay, where's your God now?" And the Jew replied quietly, "Right down here, right down here with me in this muck!"

God is not in the business of intending, causing, or tolerating human misery or natural evil, but struggles alongside human beings in alleviating it. As pastor James Callahan affirms: "Wherever we go, in hurt and sorrow and despair, God has been there first, goes with us, shows up, and is glad to be there with and for us."

A little girl once told Sophia Fahs that "God is what grows," and affirmatists would concur. But negative as well as positive things grow. Children maturing is radically different than a cancerous tumor expanding, yet panentheism implies that God is somehow mixed up in the whole of life: its pain and suffering as well.

After the second destruction of the Jewish Temple in 70 CE, Talmudic scholars, standing amidst the rubble of their own society, realized that God joined them in weeping. Evidently, the angels couldn't tolerate viewing God's immense sadness. It pained them so, and they did everything to prevent God from shedding tears. To no avail, because God's response was equally dramatic:

> *If you seek to prevent Me from crying here, I will simply find another place where you cannot approach, and cry there.*

God will not be prevented from throbbing and tears, and neither will we. Heaven and Earth weep together during life's unavoidable eddy of anguishes.

SILENCE

Our safest eloquence concerning God is our silence, when we confess that his glory is inexplicable, his greatness above our capacity and reach. He is above, and we upon earth, therefore it behooveth our words to be wary and few.

Thomas Hooker (1586-1647)

I still complain that God is silent. But I'm not as frightened of the silence as I once was. Silence is not quickly mistaken for rejection anymore. Silence is just that, silence—a different way of getting me to listen and pay attention.

Renita J. Weems

Words are wondrous vehicles, and we Unitarian Universalists will never relinquish them by descending into utter stillness and hush. Yet their fragility—indeed, inadequacy—must ever be acknowledged. The ancient Hebrews refused to write or speak the whole name of God explaining that the concept is inherently unknowable.

The hills and rivers are mute, yet they shout the wonder of deity. "To you, silence is praise" sings the Psalmist to God (65:2). There is a Hasidic saying: "The altar dearest to God is the altar of silence." The *nearest* altar as well.

Some religious folks seem to think that the number of times they mention the word *God* during conversation or worship predicts the presence of the Infinite. Hardly. One church attendee during our San Diego ministry, coming from a fundamentalist background, was initially disconcerted by the paucity of times God's name was cited in our Meeting House. After months of increasing involvement in our circle, she paid our band of freethinking mystics a high compliment: "I have never worshipped in a religious community where the 'word' God is so rarely mentioned yet the 'reality' of God so deeply felt. I now feel balanced as a Unitarian Universalist, bridging both heaven and earth. Hallelujah!" Indeed, as Marsha grew to recognize, spiritual equilibrium is the objective: where the intellect and soul, rationality and intuition are evenly affirmed.

Silence is a particularly potent and evocative lurking-place of God for verbal Unitarian Universalist types. Garrison Keillor pointedly jests: "The rule at the Unitarian monastery is complete silence, but if you think of something really good, you can go ahead and say it."

Truly, we underpractice quietude in worship and underappreciate freedom from turbulence and self-assertion at work. Our lives are prone to being cluttered with chatter, are they not? Yet periods of sufficient inwardness enable us to be receptive to otherness—be it the sounds of nature, the sounds of our own interior castle, or the sounds of divine humming.

There is the Sufi story where the governor on his travels stepped in to pay homage to the Master: "Affairs of state leave me no time for lengthy dissertations," he said. "Could you put the essence of religion into a paragraph or two for a busy person like me?" "I shall put it into a single word for the benefit of your highness." "Incredible! What is that unusual word?" "Silence." "And what is the way to Silence?" "Meditation." "And what, may I ask, is meditation?" "Silence!"

Nineteenth-century British Unitarian James Martineau claimed that words were fragile containers in conceptualizing God but ultimately needed to be used. He maintained:

> *All belief and speech respecting God is untrue yet infinitely truer than any non-belief and silence. The confession of ignorance once made, we may proceed to use such poor thought and language as we find least unsuitable to so high a matter.*

Clearly, words are essential in conceiving, then conveying, messages about anything spiritual, including the Unknown. But we dare not underrate the power and relevance of silence as an equally valuable (not lesser) vehicle for luring the Divine into our lives or us into Its sphere.

We join the Buddhists, among other seekers, who claim that the Void can furnish a worthy vessel for the sacred. Ralph Waldo Emerson, in pointing to the numinous, said: "I like the silent church before the service begins, better than any preaching." For, as he stated elsewhere: "Let us be silent, that we may hear the whispers of the Gods."

At this juncture, some comments about God's silence are in order. In fact, the Eternal Spirit has proven to be progressively quiet and uninvolved, according to Jack Myle's analysis in his book, *The Biography of God*, where he notes that in the Hebrew Bible, action yields to speech, which yields in its turn to silence. As he states it:

God's last words are those he speaks to Job, the human being who dares to challenge not his physical power but his moral authority. Within the Book of Job itself, God's climactic and overwhelming reply seems to silence Job. But reading from the end of the Book of Job onward, we see that it is Job who has somehow silenced God. God never speaks again, and he is decreasingly spoken of. In the Book of Esther—a book in which, as in the Book of Exodus, his chosen people faces a genocidal enemy—God is never so much as mentioned. In effect, the Jews surmount the threat without his help.

And in the Christian scriptures God speaks but once, to say: "This is my beloved son, in whom I am well pleased." Jesus talks a lot, but not the Creator. So God, in both the Hebrew and Christian chronicles, seems to grow gradually more reserved, if not distant—certainly mysterious.

Furthermore, there are contemporary Jews who lament not only the silence of God in the closing ten books of their holy writ but also his inscrutable nonappearance during the Holocaust. For some this state of affairs leads to passionate atheism, others are left in the clutches of agnosticism, and still other Jews, in the face of God's quietude, muster affirmations of his presence, even partnership.

In the light of God's tormenting silence, I tend to concur with Mary Virginia Micka:

It isn't that I believe God is dead, but God is so silent, has been for so long,

and is so hidden, that I take it as a sign I
must watch in other places or simply tend
my small fires until the end.

Despite what God may or may not be up to, there remains ample moral challenge for humans to pursue. Our work is fairly clear. And a portion of it is to keep our lives lubricated with adequate periods of solitude, stillness, and silence.

Entering the silence is a holy vow accessible to all God's creatures—women, men and children, animals and plants, too. The Greek root *mys* in the words mystery and mystic means shutting the eyes, ears, or mouth, because in the presence of luminous and numinous things, we are driven to silence. Truly, the sacred enterprise beckons us to be speechless and dumb sometimes, to still our mouth, then our mind, finally our will—to shut up fully before we dare to open up freshly to the bidding of the Spirit. It calls us to enter the silence, so the mystery within us might connect with the mystery beyond us.

Once the Japanese emperor Hirohito was driven to a meeting hall for a scheduled appointment. When he arrived, no one was there. The Emperor strolled into the middle of the grand hall, stood silently for several moments, then bowed to the empty space. He smiled, then told his assistants: "We must arrange more appointments like this. I haven't enjoyed myself so much for a long time." Hirohito personifies the Asian fondness for quiet inactivity as a source of restoring the spirit. Black Elk reminds us: "Is not silence the very voice of the Great Spirit?"

The Great Silence intimidates contemporary folks, so we rush to fill our solitude with social busy-ness, bodies, food and drink, TV, and miscellaneous inanities instead of mustering the courage to embrace holy emptiness.

In our wiser moments, we Unitarian Universalists adhere to Meister Eckhart's invitation: "Quit flapping your gums about God...The most beautiful thing a person can say about God would be for that person to remain silent from the wisdom of an inner wealth."

Befriending the Great Silence is a hallowed, occasionally harrowing, imperative for the religious pilgrim. One day when we cross over into our final silence, the ultimate darkness, we will be spiritually seasoned, ready to connect with Silence as God.

SURRENDER

We should sink eternally from something into
nothing, into this One...let your own being sink into
and flow away into God's being God.

—Meister Eckhart

For full enjoyment of sex, one does the same thing
one does with God—one says: "I am Thine."

—Maya Angelou

When asked by a disciple how one could experience
God, a Sufi mystic slipped off his tunic and stepped
into the pouring rain. Lying on the grass he opened
his mouth and spread his arms. "That's how," he
said.

—Bruce Marshall

Earlier in my religious adolescence I clung to God in a way that did neither of us justice. Then I rebelled against God and eased into a state of presumed self-sufficiency. Presently, although I refuse to subjugate myself to any external power, I am willing to surrender to divine mystery. As life-long Unitarian Universalist Linda Horton voices: "The idea of turning my life over to God no longer seems alien."

This process of *turning* can prove to be a valuable one. In the Hebrew scriptures, the sign of the burning bush led Moses to say: "I will turn aside and see this great sight, why the bush is not burnt." Only when God sees that Moses does in fact turn aside, turn around and take notice, does Yahweh speak to him.

In a sense, that's the way with all of us, isn't it? God supplies signs of presence and activity, both obvious and obscure, but refuses to speak to us until we make a move, show interest, turn around to see. Affirming an omen of the divine doesn't pose an effortless endeavor. It requires openness of heart and sharpness of vision. Human attention. Effort.

Robert Frost snares the twisting human-divine gambol in his poem *Not All There*:

> *I turned to speak to God*
> *About the world's despair;*
> *But to make bad matters worse*
> *I found God wasn't there.*
> *God turned to speak to me*
> *(Don't anybody laugh).*
> *God found I wasn't there—*
> *At least not over half.*

As with any relationship of value and power, we need to move forward, rather than away, to advance. This goes for forging both earthly and heavenly bonds. St. Paul reminds us in his sermon on Mars Hill, "God is not very far from each one of us." But as long as the Spirit remains but an abstract notion not a transforming power, we will freeze in our philosophical tracks and fail to risk a relational leap of faith.

There is a Hasidic tale that bolsters this line of thought:

> *The Kotzer rabbi once asked several of*
> *his disciples: "Where does God exist?"*
> *"Everywhere," the surprised disciples*

replied with alacrity. "No," said the wise rebbe, "God exists only where we let him in!"

The human-divine dance may take time and prove to be a somewhat clumsy process, but this primal relationship remains an interactive affair, requiring openness and receptivity on both sides. Humans can only be responsible for our part in the exchange, for opening our hearts and minds to let the Eternal in.

Everyday I surrender willingly to the inexplicable mysteries of vocation, marriage, and parenting. I can explain these no more conclusively than I can explain deity. Think of sexuality—a matter of allowing oneself to be profoundly vulnerable, intimate, and released into the safekeeping of one's partner. Authentic love requires treading the fine line between surrender and submission. Appropriately, the Hebrew word, *yadah*, for knowing God, is the same term used for knowing one's lover sexually. The key in surrendering to God is to enter the being of God and to allow God to enter ours—without either of us losing our respective identities. The divine-human encounter should produce a meeting not a merging.

Whatever else Ultimate Mystery might be, it surely resembles a fount of universal and limitless love, inclusive of all creatures and infinitely sympathetic. Our Universalist theology posits that love is the Alpha and Omega of existence—the Source, the Substance, and the Summit of all religious nourishment and directive. We declare that the central creational act has been God loving all beings into existence. The fundamental energy of reality is not air or water, fire or earth, as Ionian philosophy claimed, but love. Our human imperative, then, is to pass love on to all of creation during our earthly stay, to keep the gift moving.

Infused with and surrounded by abiding love, as Unitarians we cherish every unit of existence and treat it as holy, and as Universalists we exhibit a spacious love inclusive of all creatures. Through loving we fulfill our human destiny and foster connections with divine presence...we bridge heaven and earth. This is why process theologian, Henry Nelson Wieman, was led to affirm that "God is Creative Interchange."

The Hindu way of religion emphasizes three pathways to communion with Brahman: the way of *knowledge*, the way of *devotion*, and the way of *action*. Each has its own merits. Surrendering emphasizes the way of devotion: love and affectional bonding. It reminds us that seeking understandably culminates in some form of surrender, that religion is based on relationality, "deep calling unto deep" (Psalmist), requiring ample heartfulness. Or as Jeremiah stated it: "When you search for me, you will find me; if you seek me with all your heart, I will let you find me, says the Lord" (29: 12-14).

Many mystics have sought to forge a bond of intimacy rather than to apprehend God through intellectual discourse. They have successfully resisted what ethicist Edwin Vacek calls "anonymous monotheism." Mystics have commonly referred to God as their Beloved. For example, the 16th-century Indian poetess and saint, Mirabai, proclaimed, "All-pervading One, I am dyed in Your color. When other women's sweethearts live in foreign lands, they write letter after letter. But my Beloved lives in my heart, so I sing happily day and night."

Classic Unitarian Universalist adherents have majored in the ways of knowledge and action, while minoring in the pathway of devotion. We have been accustomed to defining ourselves more as seekers than finders, debaters instead of devotees—pilgrims focused on discussion rather than experience, endlessly tracking, rarely making peace with what we've found and with whom we reside. But it is my observation that we are currently learning, slowly incorporating, the values of healthy surrender into our spiritual lives.

Colleague Ernest Sommerfeld reflects on this development:

> *True believers (omit the credulous) cannot be choosers. Seekers are not responsible for what they find, but having found are accounted liable for what becomes of having mind.*

Indeed, religion is ultimately about what you do with who you are and what you possess. As such, it's finally less about knowledge and more about relationship. As Alice Walker says: "I come to church not to find God but to share God." We need sometimes to, as the recovery movement wisdom invites, "let go and let God." Not in a self-abdicating way, but in a mutually affirming one. In short, surrender, as in any mature love relationship.

Can we Unitarian Universalists envision having a close and loving connection to God? If so, what is the nature of the affectional tie? Do we allow God to be an active, controlling, or silent partner? I tend to envisage God not as a perfect senior partner but as a mystical comrade who companions me through the trials and delights and blahs of earthly travel. How about you?

The seasoned religious humanist of yesteryear, John Dietrich, put it persuasively:

> *God must be felt and experienced, rather than thought of and reasoned about. One's whole being is involved here, not the intellect alone. Out of this feeling and experience, an intimate, inward, personal relationship emerges. Awareness of mystery in the nature of things is kept alive, is repeatedly renewed in us.*

For such a mystical bond to be fostered, some level of devotion, yea surrender, is essential.

Again, in surrendering to God, the Holy One, Creative Interchange (call it what you will) submission is not required, but trust is. Indeed, the Hebrew word for faith, *bitachon*, really means trust. Surrender is about pledging our troth, our trust, forging a vow, making and keeping promises. And surrender implies that sacrifices may be in store for us. For whenever we enter a holy union with either human or divine beings, we do not emerge the same. We are eternally changed.

Surrender means "learning to free fall." This sentiment is echoed by the poetic reflection of Wendy Wright:

> *How dark the seeing. How fragmentary. Mostly it consists of learning to free fall. Learning to trust the constant*

somersaulting. Learning to live with spiritual vertigo. Learning to love the darkness. Learning to trust the brief glimpses. Learning that blindness is its own seeing. Learning that the falling is in itself beautiful. That at the bottom of the well of my heart, I free fall into You.

Surrender denotes giving ourselves over without giving ourselves away—giving ourselves to an ally with whom we can play, wrangle, and labor to co-create an evolving universe. Sometimes I call that reality God; sometimes I don't. Sometimes I choose to talk about it; others times I hold my tongue and simply revel in the hallowed embrace of partnership, or brood amidst the quietude.

And at the close of our earthly journey, we will release our beings back to the Mystery from which we came, from dust unto dust, rejoining the loving grasp of the Eternal One who tenderly brought us into being, has nurtured ever since, and will not let us go. "Rest assured"—as our Universalist forebears put it.

VI. SEVEN FUNDAMENTAL REMINDERS

We don't have to be informed so much as to be reminded.

—Samuel Johnson

There are certain reminders integral to the Unitarian Universalist way in religion that endeavor to keep our explorations into God fluid not fixed, appropriately modest not brazen, insistently honest and honorable. That is, if we pay heed to them.

REMINDER I: "God Is Larger"

God transcends all things and exceeds all intellect and mind. God is above anything that can be conceived.

—Michael Servetus (1512-1553)

God, you are so vast!

—Rainer Maria Rilke

God is transcendent—we cannot create, comprehend, or control It/Her/Him. Sara Maitland, in her perceptive volume entitled *A Big-Enough God*, puts all god-talk in proper focus:

> God is up to something larger, more complex, and more refined than we seem able to imagine. What we know of God, we know from God; and a theology that proceeds on any other terms is for me deficient...The desire to reduce it all to a

tidy little formula is irresistible and must be resisted. In the last count why bother about a tiny little, simple God who is slightly less complicated than the workings of my own mind?

I remember sharing a conversation about God with primary age children in our chapel worship one Sunday. I inquired: What does God look like? There were various answers, but the one that stuck with me that morning was: "God is fat!" After the initial shock to my adult ears, I have grown to understand, even like, that off-beat response of my 8-year-old buddy. Because God *is* fat, colossal, mammoth—a reality that incorporates all conceivable human notions but remains greater than that. Fat doesn't do God justice, but at least it's moving in the right direction—away from puniness and diminished perspective.

The Rig Veda refers to the Eternal as extending "ten fingers' breadth beyond." The Muslims say "allahu akbar," which means not "God is great!" as often translated, but "God is greater!"—greater than any particular vision or dogma or rule.

Our 16th-century Unitarian forebear, Michael Servetus, depicts God as being "above anything that can be conceived." Universalist Benjamin Rush in 1790 refers to the Supreme Being as "infinite in all his perfections...incomprehensible." Twentieth-century Unitarian Universalist theologian Bernard Loomer focused his process thought on describing a God of larger proportions than mere abstractions could achieve. He kept emphasizing the "size" of God: huge both in grandeur and in goodness.

Suffice it to say, we belong to the company of loyalists who refuse to posit a deity that is regionalized or possessible. Hence, our free faith is as expansive as the cosmos and resonates with the story of Rabbi Moshe of Kobryn who said: "When you utter a word before God, then enter into that word with every one of your limbs." One of his listeners remarked: "How can a big human being possibly enter into a little word?" "Anyone who thinks themselves bigger than the word," said the zaddik, "is not the kind of person we are talking about."

REMINDER II: We Are Humans—Neither Angels nor Gods

We do pretty well—for human beings. For we are not gods with absolute powers to manipulate the world. Nor are we gifted with pure reason which could bring perfect concepts to bear upon complex problems. We are product and part of the evolutionary process.

—John Ruskin Clark

We exist not alone. There is no rugged individualism among species. We are part of a sacred ecosystem that involves all other creatures upon Earth, the constellations, and the galaxies. We are part of an interrelated system out of which we have come, in which we live, by which are sustained. That is what must be said in our time.

—Roy Phillips

We are creatures with earthbound vision. None of us holds a god's-eye view of reality. Unitarian Universalism begins and ends by making sufficient peace with this fact. According to Jewish lore, the first two utterances of the Decalogue came straight from God, "I am the Lord your God." and "You shall have no other gods before me." These assertions produce one discernment: "I'm God, you're not."

Oliver Wendell Holmes, Jr. (1841-1935) conveyed to his buddy William James that "the great act of faith is when we decide that we are not God." Indeed, it is reported that Holmes on his 90th birthday was still reminding people that the "discovery that I was not God was truly the secret of success." Or as an African-American woman, after lengthy involvement in twelve-step programs, mused: "Honey, even if you don't believe in God, can you believe you ain't Him?"

But there is a circulating assumption, voiced today by psycho-spiritual writers today such as Marianne Williamson, that "the idea that we are separate from God is merely an illusion of consciousness." And this is indeed the persuasion of notable mystics who vouch that to enter the Numinous One is to experience the unity of all things. Such union with the Absolute often grants mystics a sense of total belonging.

However, I would submit that earthlings and deities are interweaving but distinct realities. Whereas the divine moves within and through us, we are not one and the same. Blurring the boundaries between the human and the divine realms does disservice to both.

Nonetheless, we humans remain impressive creatures. We are inescapably moral beings. There is that of the divine spark in every person...including those designated to be the very least, lost, and last among us.

At highest common denominator, we are human beings—neither angels nor gods—although there may be something of each within our bosom. Such a recognition proves both humbling and freeing.

The story is told that some years after General MacArthur and the American Occupation Forces in Japan relegated the Japanese Emperor from the status of deity to that of mere mortal, Emperor Hirohito was interviewed about the change in station. "You know," he said, "I'm really quite satisfied. You can't imagine all the extra work I had to do when I was a god."

Our culminating 7th Unitarian Universalist Principle declares: "We covenant to affirm and promote respect for the interdependent web of all existence of which we are a part." This means we are neither the whole of nor extraneous to Creation but a critical cog. Moreover, we were fashioned incomplete with the joyous responsibility of collaborating with the Creator in the furtherance of our own evolution as well as that of existence. Genetics and nature shape us, but they don't finalize us.

We are "part and parcel of the universe" (Emerson). This is our glorious challenge and sobering admonition. It is foolish either to grovel as lackeys before the Most High or conspire to storm the heavens. Things work best when we humans accompany God in contributing toward a just and beautiful cosmos.

Unitarian minister Curtis Reese from Des Moines, Iowa, stood unalterably opposed to any understanding of God that demanded that humans prostrate themselves like a serf before a feudal lord. He attacked autocratic religion but preached a democratic one wherein "humans consciously become co-workers with cosmic processes."

The mission of Unitarian Universalist religion resembles the imperative of the Hebrew prophet Micah: to "do justice, love kindness and to walk humbly with our God." Three important moves: *walking* alongside neither behind nor ahead of God; walking *humbly,* that is, with an attitude of reverence; and walking humbly *with our God*, namely, our own deity not one borrowed or inherited from elsewhere.

REMINDER III: Many Are the Pathways to God

Whatever the world may say, it must sometime become clear that God is but one.

—Francis David's last sermon (1579)

Our life is polytheistic; a many-splendored thing, down deep, if we only knew it.

—David Miller

Truth is One; the wise call it by many names.

—Rig Veda

From the origins of both Unitarianism and Universalism, we have closely identified ourselves with the posture of ethical monotheism in religious history. God for us has been moral and indivisible. We live in a unified cosmos. As David Parke phrases it:

Unitarian Universalists have a unitive vision—one life, one people, one world, one God, one suffering, one righteousness, one passage, one consummation.

But a single perception of the divine will always be too limiting for a faith as theological diverse as ours—notwithstanding the joke voiced by prominent philosopher, Alfred North Whitehead: "A Unitarian is a person who believes there is, at most, one God."

Therefore, we are beholden to the paradoxical affirmation of our forebear Ralph Waldo Emerson when he penned: "God is unity, but always works in variety." We comprise separate strands of an interdependent web. We state unequivocally in our worship services that "we are an intentionally diverse faith."

We have tolerated, nay encouraged, a plethora of routes to the sacred. We can neither experience the Universe in like manner nor describe it uniformly. A rigid monotheism can easily breed a sense of arrogance that is threatened by the presence of neighboring deities. Gary Blaine refers to our splurge of analogues for any human conversation about God:

> *Unitarian forebear, William Ellery Channing, in the **Perfect Life in Twelve Discourses,** used 75 different metonymies and metaphors to characterize God, including Infinite Spirit, Creative Mind, Supreme Power, Divine Original, Divine Character, and Heavenly Parent. The process of metaphors is a constant one of expansion and interpretation. That is the process by which truth is kept vital and relevant.*

God reflects the far-ranging, yin-yang dimensions of Reality: light and dark, male and female, soft and hard, good and evil, soil and sky. God pervades all races, genders, capacities, orientations, conditions of earthly existence. This maddening complexity of God's nature is evidenced in Hindu tradition where the five faces of Shiva are noted in dynamic tension: creator, sustainer, destroyer, mystery, and grace. Hinduism befuddles our Western religious consciousness with its multiheaded, multiarmed deities. And, of course, Islam refers to the 99 names of God.

In a nutshell, our ever-evolving Unitarian Universalist religion may best be portrayed as merging monotheistic and polytheistic sentiments in creative embrace—more precisely henotheistic since we likely choose to revere but one God at a time from among the sweep of options. But idolatry creeps in whenever we clasp a favorite metaphor or resist appreciating the image of our fellow traveler.

Indeed, monotheistic religions have all too often grown militaristic in language and social relations. Author Philip Roth counters this tendency through the voice of his character, Ozzie, in the novel *Portnoy's Complaint*: "You shouldn't hit me about God, Mama. You should never hit anybody about God. Promise me you'll never hit anybody about God."

As a Greek major in college, one of my favorite plays has Euripides closing *The Bacchae* with the words, "Many are the shapes of things divine." At core, our theologies are manifold, our paths are numerous, our symbols for the sacred are plenteous. As Brian Wren and Carleton Young's contemporary (1989) hymn in

Singing the Living Tradition posits: "Bring many names, beautiful and good, celebrate in parable and story, holiness and glory, living, loving God: hail and hosanna, bring many names." God's revelations are not merely singular, or even plural, but limitless.

REMINDER IV: God Must Be Experienced First-Hand

You yourself a newborn bard of the Holy Ghost, cast behind you all conformity, and acquaint people at first-hand with Deity.

—Ralph Waldo Emerson, essayist

To invoke God as a blanket explanation of the unexplained is to make God the friend of ignorance. If God is to be found, it must surely be through what we discover about the world, not what we fail to discover.

—Paul Davies, physicist

The world is charged with the grandeur of God.

—Gerard Manley Hopkins, poet

Emerson in his Harvard Divinity School address (1838) was goading ministerial students to nudge future parishioners to experience the Infinite Presence directly. As he phrased it elsewhere: "The divine can be experienced in the immediacy of existence." If truth be told, Unitarian Universalism has always prodded its devotees to make first-hand connection with Deity, be it through reason or the senses, intuition or empiricism. There exists no divine reality "above" or "beyond" or "below" this world that doesn't necessitate a processing through our human senses and soul, however frail and flawed.

Thomas Merton claimed that "knowledge of God just can't be passed down from parent to child!" What he meant was that it must be earned—each of us must engage in our own inimitable wrestling match with Yahweh. As Unitarian Universalists we hold that religion is more a matter of heresy (choice-making) than inheritance (borrowing). Early wisdom must be amended as we mold our tomorrows.

There are believers who would call themselves fideists, believing in God for personal or pragmatic reasons. Renown skeptic Martin Gardner is one such affirmatist. Along with Miguel Unamuno he contends that atheists have better arguments than theists, but he still holds to the position of *credo consolans,* "I believe because it is consoling."

Such thinking proves inadequate for most Unitarian Universalists. However comforting our individual faith needs to be, it must also be grounded in sufficient evidence. Not absolute but enough data. Our leaps must be ones not of credulity but of reasonableness. Our devotion dare not be blind. Reason, while imperfect, comprises a necessary tool in explicating the depths of holiness. As Charles Hartshorne mused:

> *About the age of seventeen, after reading Emerson's Essays, I made up my mind to trust reason to the end....which brought me to reject the widespread contention that the deepest questions simply elude the rational process, concluding instead*

*that ultimate concepts have a rational
structure that is lucid and intellectually
beautiful.*

Perhaps no one has blended religion and science more adeptly than the French field paleontologist, Teilhard de Chardin, who traversed the globe to hunt for fragments of human ancestors, contending that every fossilized bone and flake of stone excavated from the earth was a clue to God's plan of creation. As Chet Raymo in his book *Skeptics and True Believers: The Exhilarating Connection Between Science and Religion* asserts:

> *De Chardin looked for the completion of
> evolution in a kind of cosmic
> consciousness—the Omega, he called it—
> that he identified with God. He insisted
> that the truest knowledge of creation is
> that provided by contemporary science.
> Late in life he wrote to a friend: "Less
> and less do I see any difference now
> between research and adoration."*

Because of our bias toward first-hand observation, Unitarian Universalism has always concurred with Albert Einstein, who argued that "Science without religion is lame, and religion without science is blind." Certainly, each is incomplete in itself, representing but a portion of our human potential.

But their differences, while documented, should not be exaggerated. It's no longer fair or accurate to declare that science focuses on *facts* and religion on *meanings*. And science doesn't simply deal with the *objective* any more than religion operates in the *subjective* realm alone. These disciplines constantly shuttle back and forth.

Imaginative pioneers in both science and religion respect one another, converse with, borrow from, and labor alongside one another. Neither claims to be either omniscient or infallible. In the eternal pursuit of Truth and Holiness they are full-fledged partners—exchanging values and proffering criticisms.

Both religion and science are conceived in curiosity, standing in awe and humility before the unspeakable grandeur and complexity of the universe—a cosmos bigger than our brains, just as God is greater than our grasp.

It is said that science was born when the philosopher or religionist rolled up his or her sleeves. One such pioneer, Joseph Priestley, a British Unitarian minister, discovered oxygen and the process of carbonation of water, even called himself "an experimental philosopher."

So, true science entails faith, launching with certain hypotheses about the underlying nature of the real world. Albert Einstein was a scientist who considered himself a mystic as well. He noted, "I didn't arrive at my understanding of the fundamental laws of the universe through my rational mind." Indeed, science cannot prove the existence of God, let alone spy the deity at the end of a telescope. But to some believers, probing the universe certainly delivers clues about what God might be like.

Embedded within our liberal religious heritage is a stance known to many as scientific theology. Henry

Nelson Wieman, a liberal Baptist who later in life became a Unitarian, constructed a process philosophy undergirding for a rigorous empirical theology that accordingly paved the road to salvation.

Unitarian Universalist minister John Ruskin Clark conceived of God neither as a personal deity nor as a metaphysical abstraction but as the *Great Living System*—an objective, unified moral law, the Body of God, to be explored and honored, even glorified. Clark's paradigm reminds one of Stephen Hawking's natural theology, wherein God's mind is equivalent to a plan of creation of remarkable simplicity, the so-called *Grand Unified Theory,* shared by countless contemporary physicists.

Therefore, to grasp the Holy, we must experience the universe upclose and personal. Often we are taught that our bodies are fragments of the universe...pieces completely detached from the rest, handed over to us to inhabit. We get caught in this state of disconnection rather than connection with the earth. We have even been told to believe that we humans hold dominion over the soil and sky, animals and plants. Yet, as we Unitarian Universalists profess, humans are summoned to be partners in the evolution of the cosmic "interdependent web."

We must get to know the earth as one body would know another and dwell respectfully in one another's embrace.

REMINDER V: God Is Transpersonal Yet...

My experiential reality is a paradox. The Divine demand which I experience in the depths of my being is for all of creation to be healed and unfolded in its potential. I cannot translate that into a personally loving God. Yet it does seem to address me personally. I do believe that something irrepressible in the deep ecology of the Universe cries out on behalf of those who need redress or healing, on behalf of all growing and creative things, and that there is something of mystery in me which responds.

—Linda Smith Horton

I found god in myself/and I loved her/I loved her fiercely.

—Ntozake Shange

Since God surpasses human grasp, it is more suitable to speak of God in nonpersonal terms, employing phrases like Tillich's "ground of being," St. Teresa of Avila's "supplier of true life," Karl Rahner's "holy mystery," or Rosemary Ruether's "matrix surrounding and sustaining all life." Although Hebrew has no neuter pronoun, in Sanskrit, the ancient Hindus referred to the Eternal Spirit as both *It* and *That.* St. Augustine referred to God as "that which is."

Notwithstanding, for many believers, the qualities we ascribe to deity—justice, faithfulness, compassion, and the like—are incorrigibly personal and parallel our human world more often than not. The Eternal, while transpersonal, is mediated through personal hints and encounters, thus spawning yet another infuriating paradox to be ridden as Unitarian Universalists.

Xenophanes, one of the Pre-Socratic Greek philosophers, said that any god of the horses would undoubtedly be horse-like, any god of the fish, fish-like; and any god of human beings, human-like or personal. Try as we may, we can never really rise above quasi-anthropomorphic articulations of Transcendence.

It's downright humbling for humans to acknowledge that whenever we talk about God, the results resemble us. Our qualities. Our aspirations. Our flaws. Our evolution. The deity that purportedly created us is fabricated in our own assorted images. Zorba the Greek put it baldly: "I think of God as being exactly like me. Only bigger, stronger, crazier. And immortal, into the bargain!"

So we turn to God as another You or Thou—to be engaged rather than used, since, as Martin Buber reminds us, ultimate reality cannot be expressed, only addressed. Buber goes on to assert that the origin of the divine name *Yahweh* means roughly "O the One!" In short, God cannot be named, merely exclaimed. A sobering reminder for seekers to stay clear of attempts at definition.

There is noticeable loss in describing God as Ground or Substance or Matrix, when we humans long to connect with God through an intimate "I-Thou" bond. Nonetheless, we must be sobered by the fact that believing in the personal deity of the Hebrew or

Christian scriptures can lead to subtle, self-centered manipulative behavior that isn't as likely with an impersonal reality like Brahman.

A related paradox arises when we consider God's gender. Unitarian Universalists attempt to be ambidextrous, affirming both feminine and masculine energies and demeanors as valid descriptors of the nature of the Universe. Karen Armstrong notes "that in Arabic *al-Lab* (the supreme name for God) is grammatically masculine, but the word for the divine and inscrutable essence of God, *al-dhat,* is feminine." Furthermore, in Hindu theological lore, Shiva (male) and Shakti (female) are inseparably linked.

World religions utilize several female metaphors for God, prompting us that gender equity is imperative on both the divine and human planes. God and Goddess are equally valued deities; likewise, male and female are uniformly worthwhile earthlings. Theological and political justice are interwoven.

Unitarian Universalists have wrestled mightily with engendered and degendered accounts of the Holy. This is amply referenced in the quotations and literature annotated in the appendix. In sum, we resonate with the wisdom of our Unitarian foresister Julia Ward Howe when she proclaimed:

> *I think nothing is religion which puts one*
> *individual absolutely above another, and*
> *surely nothing is religion which puts one*
> *sex above another.*

We liberal religionists confess that no single deity can resemble everyone. After all, at the core of earth-based spirituality lies the story of Mother Earth and Father Sky, from whose passionate union emerges all living entities. Therefore, we choose to honor the diversity of divinity, and the divinity of diversity— women and men and transgendered folks, all ages and races, capacities and orientations, classes and theological preferences.

Beneath the objective or subjective nature of divinity, beyond Its and Thous, lies the spiritual. Kinship between heaven and earth is fully restored when we affirm that all living beings are infused with soul/spirit—humans, animals, and deities alike.

Now, there exist psychologists as well as religionists who would distinguish between **soul** (having to do with depth and descent) and **spirit** (focusing upon height and ascent). However, the Eternal moves nimbly both in the bottommost regions as well as the heavens, so I leave it to each Unitarian Universalist pilgrim to contour distinctions suitable for your own personal journey.

I would only remind us that an upbeat, enlightened religion such as ours frequently bypasses digging about in the dark, dank, dirty netherworld of our souls. We are prone to avoid or suppress what Robert Bly calls "the road of ashes, where we learn to shudder and shed tears." A blend of rationalism and stoicism often makes descent into the shadowy sphere of our psyches scary. But go there we must.

We are charged to be balanced seekers—tilling the humus as well as sailing the skies. We live as trees: growing both up and down simultaneously, with a huge canopy of branches above and an unseen but vast system of roots below, with our trunks linking and separating these two complex networks. Both soul and spirit work are critical avenues to experiencing the Divine. 117

A few reflections upon God as Soul, then as Spirit.

Emerson refers to God as the Eternal One or Unity or Over-Soul, within which our human being is contained and connected. It is tempting to hunt for God all over creation and bypass inklings of the divine lodged within our own souls. When the New Testament asserts that "the realm of God dwells *entos* us," the Greek word entos refers to both *among* us (amid life's communal realities) and *within* us (within our interior chambers). Religion proves both a solidary and a solitary adventure.

Whenever our minds cannot produce an adequate bond with God or our hearts are disjointed from divinity, it is often deep within our very souls that the sacred can be felt. Our ecstatic encounters with God or Brahman or Allah (or whatever name we may give) are singular and private, yet can be shared, soul to soul, with other sisters and brothers.

A. Powell Davies, a Unitarian pastoral leader in our nation's capitol in the 1950s, asserted that "the purpose of life is to grow your soul." So it is, and as we earthlings pursue the maturation of our souls, we grow in deeper kinship with the Eternal One.

God is also depicted as Spirit, the Great Spirit as the Native Americans would put it, and our mission is to be on good terms with this source of unlimited energy. Spirit is equatable with breath—a reality central to both human existence and divine activity.

Paying attention to our breath is a hallowed enterprise: indeed, it is the heart of meditation practiced the universe over. Breathing deeply places us in touch with the Source of Life, the animating energy that infuses the entirety of creation. As we breathe, we share God.

For Unitarian Universalists, the holy spirit is not a triune entity but a presence that permeates all human encounters. Such holiness of spirit comforts and challenges us at every corner. However, we must never forget that the spirit, like the wind, bloweth where it will (the Gospel of John). We experience its force but cannot contain or pin it down.

Lest we overspiritualize our religion, another paradox emerges. We support Sallie McFague and other ecological theologians in "interpreting creation as all the myriad forms of matter bodied forth from God and empowered with the breath of life, the spirit of God."

It is no surprise that God must be continually referenced with an interweaving mix of spiritual and physical metaphors.

REMINDER VI: God Must Remain Wild

*Offer to God an acceptable worship with reverence
and awe; for indeed our God is a consuming fire.*

—Hebrews 12:28-29

*Throughout the Jewish and Christian traditions
prophetic thinkers have challenged the propensity
of the human heart to evade the living God by
taming the wildness of divine mystery into a more
domesticated deity.*

—Elizabeth Johnson

*Anybody can love a nice god; it's loving the truth
about God and the devil that is difficult.*

—Jacob Needleman

You can't tame God, who's wild, you know.

—C. S. Lewis

In Paul Tillich's formative days as a professor at Harvard, students would pack his lectures in Emerson Hall. Someone told the German-born theologian that with his being on the faculty, it was now "safe and respectable" to mention the word God. Tillich, in dismay, replied, "You forget that God is a consuming fire!" As Unitarian Universalist minister David Johnson concludes: "Whatever else God may be, God is not a household pet, domesticated, a comfortable companion, comprehended, caught in the narrow net of our understandings or expectations."

Every god of any self-respecting religion is portrayed more as a consuming fire than as a candle flame—a blaze that devours even as it purifies. Mature religion refuses to trivialize God into a serviceable Being who nestles in our arms or harkens to our every whim. Engaging the Infinite Spirit remains a *mysterium terribile et fascinans.*

Throughout history, believers have feverishly tried to convert God into a congenial cohort, placing him squarely in their camp in personal dispute or international strife. A group of church leaders came to President Lincoln one day saying that they were quite sure, after prayer, that God was on their side. Lincoln gave them the kind of answer they loathed yet deserved: "I am not so much concerned as to whether or not God is on my side. What I am concerned with is making sure that I am on God's side." Or as colleague, Bob Doss, signs all his letters: "Vamos con Dios" meaning "let us go, be or connect with God" rather than the other way around.

Too much religion has been a brash attempt to garner God's approval for our plans and allegiance to our prejudices through all kinds of shenanigans, but evolved religion knows better. It recognizes that the primary purpose of existence is to give love as an activity rather than receive love as a commodity. Unitarian Universalist minister Webster Kitchell understands this mission:

> *The crux of religion for me is how to love God. There are lots of activities that express love for God: meditation on the universe, making life better for all living organisms, creating artifacts that reflect the beauty of the cosmos. We do all of these things both inside and outside our church. I am willing to call these tasks the human activity of loving God.*

But no matter what we say and do, the Divine remains elusive. Nineteenth-century Unitarian forebrother Henry David Thoreau reinforces God's enigmatic and baffling nature:

> *Let God alone if need be. Methinks, if I loved him more, I should keep him, I should keep myself rather, at a more respectful distance. It is not when I am going to meet God, but when I am just turning away and leaving God alone, that I discover that God is. I say God, I am not sure that that is the name.*

Thoreau waits for God to make initial moves, then, upon greeting the divine, is cautious even to grant the encountered One a name. Thoreau was a devout panentheist, who believed that God was discoverable in the midst of all sorts of living realities and inanimate objects. There was no question that for Thoreau, the universe was riddled with evidences of holiness, but he maintained a conscious reserve in discussing it.

Such verbal shyness and modesty about God appeals to Unitarian Universalists far more than the oily chumminess with which myriad faithful relate to divine mystery. For traditional devotees, God oft-resembles a cozy, on-call, companion who panders to every entreaty or whine. But the Great Spirit will not be manipulated with sanctimonious, self-serving prayers. The Creator cannot and will not be reduced to bumper stickers and lampshade slogans.

All this should come as no surprise to earthlings. For animals need to roam wild. We humans need to remain unfettered on the pathway toward enlightenment. God is no different, says Thoreau. God covets private, open space. Like running water, God yearns to flow free and natural.

Therefore, Thoreau urges greedy, grasping Westerners to maintain "a more respectful distance" from the Source of all existence. For if we would engage the Eternal with reverence and thanksgiving, then we must allow God to be God, to be alone.

With a playful yet cutting touch, Thoreau recommends elsewhere in his writings, that if humans are really desperate for fellowship, they should spend their time befriending the devil: "God is alone but the devil is far from being alone; it sees a great deal of company; the devil is legion."

The fierce paradox obtains: when we religious pilgrims don't pressure or even pursue God, when we let God alone, the divine presence may just pay us an expected visit.

REMINDER VII: God Is Supreme Mystery

*God of unfathomable depths and unapproachable
heights, it is through mystery that you come closest
to us, and through awe that we come closest to you.*

—Ted Loder

*One Unitarian Universalist minister suggested that
we are prophets of the strangeness of God! I like
that notion. For it is precisely the strangeness and
mystery of things which calls forth an awareness of
a category beyond categories. Mystery may be the
one absolute!*

—Linda Smith Horton

Mystery may disclose itself in omens and hints, now and again, but is never fully deciphered. Mystery demands recognition. Mystery poses itself, touches us. Our response is neither to ignore it nor figure it out but wrestle mightily with it, knowing that Ultimate Mystery, known as God, remains even when all life-problems will have been solved. God, unlike a mystery novel, cannot be decoded.

In fact, Freeman Dyson, professor emeritus at the Institute for Advanced Study at Princeton, in his Templeton Prize acceptance speech, warns all god-questers of the temptation to ensnare the Eternal either in brilliant words or breakthrough discoveries:

> *Don't imagine that our latest ideas about
> the Big Bang or the human genome have
> solved the mysteries of the universe or
> the mysteries of life. As Francis Bacon,
> one of the founders of modern science,*

*almost 400 years ago, said: "The subtlety
of nature is greater many times over than
the subtlety of the senses and
understanding."*

Those are sobering yet necessary words coming from the pen of a most able empiricist.

In the first-rate volume *Does God Exist: The Great Debate,* edited by J. P. Moreland and Kai Nielsen, useful distinctions are ventured:

*First, a mystery is "not an unexplorable
and unintelligible question, but one in
which the questioner is personally and
inextricably involved...Death, evil,
suffering, and love are mysteries. The
number of atoms in the sun, how to cure
cancer, and whether Shakespeare wrote
Shakespeare are problems. How to make
people good is a mystery; how to kill
them is a problem...A second
characteristic of a mystery is that it is
deep, profound, inexhaustible, impossible
to completely illuminate...In sum,
mysteries are dark to us because they are
in us.*

Organized religion has customarily been concerned with mastery over mystery—reducing Life, Spirit, God to creedal phrases and clever doctrines. Such an approach reminds one of the philosopher and theologian who bump into an inevitable argument. The theologian says, "A philosopher is just like a blind person, in a dark room, looking for a black cat, that isn't there." "Yes," replies the philosopher, "but a theologian would find it."

In fact, there are orthodox theologians who claim closure on any and all mystery. Conversely, there are other religions who major in the exotic and esoteric. They dwell in muddled thinking and obfuscation. Clarity is apparent only to the initiated. Such occultists bask in secrecy. Mysticism devolves into magic or mystification.

Another danger is arid rationalism, wherein the universe is scrubbed clean of its imponderables and life is shrunk to the logical and literal. Unitarian Universalism aims to be a faith that neither explains away nor drowns in mysteries. Our religion pushes our minds as far as they can go, then spurs us to bow before the mysteries.

Furthermore, we recognize that Life's deeper mysteries are profoundly ambiguous. Double-sided, they attract and repel. The mysteries of creation, love, death, nature, and God are uncanny and elicit a special feeling, best rendered by the English word "awe" and its derivations "awesome" and "awful." Indeed, the wonder we experience in the presence of the Sacred is reinforced by the fact that the "ah" sound is present in the name of most deities: Adonai, Yahweh, Allah, God, Rama, Shiva, Krishna.

Those who are content to encounter rather than solve divine mystery affirm that God is but a symbol or sign pointing to unfathomable realities beyond naming. Tillich declares that "God is a symbol for God." Universalist Clarence Skinner talks of "God—majestic symbol for the sublimest reality which the human mind can conceive. Therefore, let us fill the word till it runs over with the holy associations of saints and seers, prophets and poets."

Symbols carry power when seen as pointers not idols. Ricky Hoyt, another pilgrim within our fold, confesses simply that "the term God is pointing where I want to look."

Indubitably, mystery remains central to our Unitarian Universalist manner of religion. We refuse to imprison the vast and exploding marvel of infinity in shapely statues or petrified symbols. The atheists among us declare that the endless mystery that surrounds us is puzzling, perhaps even meaningless; the agnostics perceive it to be fathomless and unknowable but not to be ignored; the affirmatists celebrate ultimate mystery as a treasure-trove of insight and direction, perhaps deigning to call it God.

Our mission as "freethinking mystics with hands" is to engage life, meet death, surrender to love, wrestle with God. Blessed are those who rather than avoiding or explaining mystery have the courage to explore its perplexity and power, from beginning to end. Blessed, indeed.

EPILOGUE

Very early I knew that the only object in life was to grow. I was often false to this knowledge, in idolatries of particular objects or impatient longings for happiness, but I have never lost sight of it, have always been controlled by it, and this first gift of thought has never been superseded by a later love.

—Margaret Fuller

God is the growth of meaning and value in the world.

—Henry Nelson Wieman

However many more breaths are left me to breathe, to aspire and conspire, I know that with my final breath I will be in the middle of learning yet another life lesson. That makes life all the more precious.

—Jane Bramadat

Recall the Latin phrase that epitomized the spirit of our 16th-century Unitarian forebears: *semper reformanda,* which means "always evolving." Membership in a responsibly free faith requires us to keep dancing, keep growing our soul, keep current and fluid our connections with divinity. Our tradition calls us to maintain doggedness instead of manufacturing dogmas. As Unitarian Universalist minister Judith Walker-Riggs couches it:

> *The universe is always changing. This gives me freedom in my religion. I no longer need to look for, nor expect to*

find, the final absolute truth, for even if I could get hold of it at this very moment, it would be gone when the universe changed again in the next. Since the universe always changes, the truth about it must change, too. So I need not be ashamed, or terrified, when my own religious vision changes. It'll just be me, being part of the universe. Could the universe itself, in all its changing, teach us that security lies not in stasis, but in process?

Yes, it could and it does.

One of Adlai Stevenson's favorite stories depicts a seven-year-old girl busy with her crayons. Her mother asked whose picture she was drawing. "God," the little girl replied. "But, my dear, nobody knows how God looks," the mother admonished. "They will when I'm finished," the child answered.

Well, neither juvenile nor elder Unitarian Universalists can claim to produce a finished portrait of the indescribable Eternal Spirit, but such a realization won't curb our ardor for drawing. We liberal religionists are, as Dianne Arakawa notes, "basically reconstructive. Our faith involves moving to a position of openness, of free inquiry, and a continuing commitment to seek the truth wherever it may lead."

If we stay awake and purposive, we will keep evolving all the way to the grave. As rabbi David Wolpe states: "Being formed in the image of God means that there is in us the infinite capacity for growth, that we can never exhaust our ability to stretch ourselves spiritually." *Stretch* is a fitting word, because as poet Marge Piercy puts it: "Loving leaves stretch marks." The process of sincerely loving ourselves, our neighbors, the natural world, and divine mystery...will unquestionably stretch us—today, tomorrow, forever.

Unitarian Universalists aver that life is ever-changing, so are human beings, so is God. We contend that every hour of our journey holds some deepening affirmation, some correcting discipline, some incredible surprise. We are born over and over again, not just once or twice. Then we die somewhere in the middle of our voyage, ready to be born yet again.

One of the more dramatic 20th-century illustrations of theological evolution within our Unitarian Universalist ranks is the story of John Dietrich. One of the 34 original signers of the "Humanist Manifesto" in 1933, Dietrich migrated over the years from humanism to theism. As he put it in 1953:

> *The manifesto seemed too narrow in its conception of the great cosmic scheme... we should not have drawn such a hard and fast distinction between theism and humanism, making them contradictory. That was all right so far as orthodox theology and supernaturalism were concerned, but there is a type of theism which does not stand in opposition to humanism, and I have come to accept that type.*

It matters not whether we modify our theology from atheism to agnosticism, or from agnosticism to affirmatism, or any alteration thereof. The central point holds: as Unitarian Universalists we are undergirded in the changing of our minds. *Semper reformanda* is our primal watchword and cry.

We are in accord with Christian biblical scholar, John A. T. Robinson, when he asserted:

> *The cry of creation itself, of which Paul speaks in Romans is of God's Spirit within us—and indeed within all nature— calling us constantly out of ourselves and beyond ourselves in order to be ourselves.*

Upon encountering the burning bush in Hebrew scriptures, Moses asks God for God's moniker, but the latter only responds with *ehyeh-asher-ehyeh,* which is oft-misrendered by the inert English, "I am who I am." In truth, the phrase translates: "I will be who I will be." Hence, God boldly claims to be an unfinished being. Listen to how rabbinical activist Michael Lerner envisions the meaning of the Hebrew deity and our concomitant human mission:

> *What the word Yahweh really means is "the transformation of the present into that which can and should be in the future." In this sense, God is the Power of Healing and Transformation in the universe and the Voice of the Future calling us to become who we need to become.*

Not only do we humans develop, so does the Infinite One, an unfixed and adaptable Being as well. Our ministerial predecessor in San Diego, John Ruskin Clark, went to the heart of the matter: "There is a presupposition that God is unchanging. But it is the nature of a vital organism to grow and change. Therefore, I believe that even the Supreme Being is constantly developing. God is not a static being but a growing organism."

Teilhard de Chardin goes so far as to insist that human evolution is our explicit purpose on earth. "Each of us is evolving towards the God-head." What do you think? Are we humans and deities growing in our own distinct ways and places or are we maturing toward a common, shared destiny? Or are both possibilities true?

Well, it's time to sum up this meandering discourse. For me it starts, persists, and ends in Love. Theologian Abraham Joshua Heschel affirmed that "God speaks slowly in our lives, a syllable at a time." Moreover, it's not until we reach the close of life, he continued, that we can read the sentence backward. And if I'm not mistaken, the sentence is astoundingly simple: Ultimate reality is infused with love.

Holding to the critical gifts of our atheism, agnosticism, and affirmatism we love God as wholeheartedly as proves reasonable. Unless we succumb to premature hardening of our spiritual arteries, we will argue with heaven all the way home. But the good news intrinsic to our life-affirming religion is that, as Thomas Carlyle remarked: "Life is one long quarrel with God, but we make up in the end."

Well, to be painstakingly honest, some of us will reconcile and some of us may never do so. And, for others, the divine-human connection will remain annoyingly half-baked, perhaps partially broken. All I'm urging, from the bottom of my Unitarian Universalist heart, is that we aspire to keep our arguing with heaven...current, honest, and respectful!

APPENDIX

UNITARIAN UNIVERSALIST QUOTES

Whether atheist, agnostic, affirmatist—or imaginative combinations thereof—most Unitarian Universalists entertain a serious (not grim) lover's quarrel with God. What follows comprises a representative survey of 20th-century statements, balanced equally among sisters and brothers, composed from both pew and pulpit—the bulk of whom are yet tilling the vineyards as "freethinking mystics with hands," still carrying on their own singular "arguments with heaven."

No commentary is furnished, since these soulful assertions carry their own power. Remember, with pride and gratitude, that these comprise spiritual relatives who share the same evolving heritage of Unitarian Universalism. May their measured claims and yearnings prove evocative as you navigate your own "awful rowing toward God."

Pagans they were called, those Greeks and Romans, Minoans and Canaanites, Egyptians and Old Europeans who worshipped Goddesses. As a woman, I need to claim that heritage. I need to know that great civilizations were created by people who worshipped the divine as female. If the myths of a culture reflect its social arrangements, women must have had power and respect. The myths tell us that in very early times the Goddess reigned.

—Shirley Ann Ranck

*To put it most starkly, we have been created by a
process in which we have now, in turn, become
creators ourselves. The divine urge of creation has
become personal in us. The evolutionary network of
ecological development, the God whom our ancestors worshipped as Loving Creator, this great God
has become conscious and self-aware in us.*

—Dwight Brown

*I find the sources of my struggle to live religiously
in the cracks between what I know and the limit of
my consciousness. One gap is between my lived life
and my knowledge of the wholeness that embraces
me and the Other, between what I experience as
limit and further possibility. I am growing at the
edge where I have to discover a sure way back to
remembering that I am not outside of God but part
of God.*

—Barbara J. Pescan

*Religious liberals welcome to their churches and
societies all those who are serious in their search
for truth: atheist or theist, Christian, Jew, Buddhist
or freethinker, who value serious re-thinking of religion and who dedicate themselves to the great
ethical ideals which have always been divine and
sacred to sensitive persons.*

—Richard E. Sykes

*Many of us claim to be seekers after the truth. But
theists believe that this truth, this ultimate reality,
seeks us with a greater intensity than we could ever
bring to bear on it. It has been said that if we take
one step towards God, God takes ten steps towards
us.*

—Barbara Merritt

Our moral and spiritual side is an aspect of the nature of the universe just as our physical hungers are, which suggests that Nature has a spiritual character and potential...this kind of humanism is actually a religion. It ties us to our home–the natural universe—with bonds of love, gratitude, and dependence, and it makes room for the unknown, which still and always surrounds us, despite all the achievements of human knowledge and the discoveries of science.

—Peter Samsom

Since one of the basic tenets of feminism is inclusiveness, it follows that I am committed to pluralism. Besides being a feminist, I am a Universalist, a Unitarian, a theist, a humanist, a Christian, an ecologist, and an existentialist. I manage all this because I have faith in, and feel responsible to, a process that transcends human values.

—Marjorie Newlin Leaming

I am an unrepentant liberal. If the gods of yesterday are dying, I am willing that they die. For there is a God who never dies, the one and only living God whose face is ever set towards tomorrow. And for those who follow where he leads, the winds of morning are already blowing, and however long the night may linger, the day of triumph is in sight.

—A. Powell Davies

It has always seemed evident to me that we live in an indifferent universe. It is up to us to make of it what we can. The only thing God adds to this situation is a wish that somebody stronger than ourselves is making things go well for us in the long run. The real negative of God is that we give up our

responsibility to make this earth a good place to
live.

—Carol Wintermute

I don't believe it is crucial that you share my faith
that it is God, as the Creative Power in the uni-
verse, that effects the transformation when, in part-
nership, we create the conditions. I do believe that
it is crucial that we share a common commitment to
create those conditions...If we share that mission,
transformation will take place and we can allow
each other the freedom to use or not use the name
of God in giving thanks.

—Edward Frost

What humanity needs now, if it—and the planet—
are to survive, is an acknowledgment of our total
ecological interdependence, coupled with an intel-
lectually honest reverence for uncertainty, an abil-
ity to live in the world as companions-in-quest, as it
were. What Unitarian Universalists have long
claimed as a methodological imperative in religion
is proving to be what is most called for in the light
of modern science: the unfolding search, rather
than the once-and-for-all identified goal, is the very
nature of what is real.

—M. Maureen Killoran

Is agnosticism enough? Agnosticism is not the de-
nial of anything; it is the acknowledgment of fini-
tude. We all need the humility of agnosticism. Of
course we cannot comprehend an infinite universe!
And yet I say that agnosticism is not enough. I want
to push the search. I want some answers...God
means for me that in life and in death no spiritual

or moral energy, no love or compassion or heroism,
is ever wasted.

—Dana MacLean Greeley

Across the spectrum of Unitarian and Universalism
we have people who call God by many different
names, and by none. But we all share a sense that
there are things worthy of our ultimate concern: the
plight of humanity, the fate of the earth and cosmos,
the quality of our relationships. In this ultimate con-
cern for the quality of the communities we create
lies the transcendent reference that will create a
strong covenant for us.

—Roberta Finkelstein

Listen, people. How could I ever prove God to you?
How can a fish prove the sea or the river in which it
swims? It is there. The fish swims in it. How could I,
with my less-than-gigantic mind prove the greatness
of God? Even King David, with all his alleged
teachings and great wisdom, only sang the praises
of God. He never embarked on a course of proving
God to others.

—Jan Vickery Knost

Feminist theology is a process in which we relate
with the sacred which permeates all of creation. It
is the stuff of daily existence as well as the visions
of how life might be. In relationships with the sa-
cred, we are transformed and we are transformers.
To touch the sacred and transform the sacred
means to bring wholeness where there is broken-
ness, discord where there is complacency, and jus-
tice where there is oppression.

—Adele Smith

The Great Surmise says simply this: At the heart of all creation lies a good intent, a purposeful goodness, from which we come, by which we live our fullest, to which we shall at last return. And this is the supreme reality of our lives.

—Carl Scovel

I don't think Unitarian Universalists are ready to give up on the notion of God or what I prefer to call the holy. We continue to examine our spirits, question the feelings we have about ourselves in relation to the earth and to fellow beings. This is the theological legacy we leave for future Unitarian Universalists—the god of the interdependent web—or the holy as experience in being a part of the interdependent web.

—Dillman Baker Sorrells

This power which I cannot explain or know or name I call God. God is not God's name. God is my name for the mystery that looms within and arches beyond the limits of my being. Life force, spirit of life, ground of being, these too are names for the unnamable which I am now content to call my God.

—F. Forrester Church

I know in my heart that God will take the form and the aspect that I need of God, and God will always give me the power to do justice. I have only to turn to God, the God I will never comprehend with my mind, and God will never let me down as along as I seek to do justice and do love.

—Elizabeth Ellis-Hagler

God, to me, is the Spirit of a spiritual universe in which all life shares an associated and interdepend-

ent destiny. God is the glorious sum of the living process, in which I, as a person, live, strive, and die. God is the existence I share with all that is or is to be.

—Jack Mendelsohn

God is the word I use to allude to that source of wonder and mystery that I experience when I contemplate the fact of my existence. I would call God—the spiritual evolution of the cosmos— creation flowing free. God is the unfolding, the potentiality, the newness. God is not the answer to the mystery of life, so much as the acknowledgment of the mystery.

—Ann Fields

Whether people call themselves theists or atheists, the issue comes down to this: What is sacred? What is truly sovereign? What is ultimately reliable? These are the questions that are involved in every discussion of the love of God. And even if we do not like to use the words "the love of God," we will nevertheless deal with these questions in any discussion of the meaning of human existence.

—James Luther Adams

They say the face of God can blind you. The arms of God, it seems, can rub you raw. And the heart of God, can break your own, so large is it, expanding. When you exercise the spirit, the soreness may remain for days, just as with the body, but it is source of health and the path of wisdom. And today I choose it one more time.

—Anita Farber-Robertson

Often theists and atheists seem offended by the other's position, as though somehow it had been adopted merely to insult them. To overcome this, we must learn not only to be honest ourselves but to accept each other's honesty, whatever our theological perspective. We must learn from each other.

—Ken Phifer

How do you prove God? How do you prove love? It can only be proved by the evidence of its presence; by the witnessing acts that convey the assurance that lets one feel loved. One feels God...and then one knows.

—Marni Harmony

I celebrate the human impulse, not in antagonism to the divine, but embodying the divine in human form and extending the divine intention to those persons, families and communities which, apart from us, would languish and die. The human and the divine are, I hold, complementary realms, interdependent and mutually reinforcing. Each exemplifies, extends, and enhances the other.

—David Parke

This changed philosophy that I believe is slowly developing in our time, and that may help us to become more integrated persons again, is not only a realistic humanism. It is also a realistic naturalism. It may even be called a realistic natural theism; but it cannot be equated simply with a belief in one God, nor with a belief in an intellectual abstraction. It is more than words can describe. It is a feeling of being a part of a Universal Living Unity.

—Sophia Fahs

It is not that I am wed to the word "God"; what is of concern to me is that I be a religious person. To be religious is to be tethered to trust, bold in pursuit of justice, and grateful for grace. For me the word "God" is a useful way of signaling all of that—of reminding me that love is transforming, that Creation is a blessing, and that sometimes at twilight the mountains have wings.

—William Schulz

My identification with divinity, the resolution of a primary religious anger and sadness, has allowed me to affirm the religious perspectives of those who do not, who have chosen not to know, or who have not experienced the "Goddess Process." It has also allowed me to blend my love of nature with a love of humanism, and to blend all this into a faith that nurtures and embraces me. At home in my study, to remind me of my journey to wholeness through the Goddess, I have an altar that is filled with Her presence—images of the Goddess. I keep these near, to remind me of the Goddess and the celebration of womanself that she has to offer. I touch and hold them for inspiration and support, and each small figure feeds and strengthens me.

—Denise D. Tracy

God is like the ocean. It is real, powerful, implacable. It is a source of beauty and pleasure and food. It can wreck ships and hills with neither remorse nor malevolence. It is in constant motion and ever-changing.

—Brandoch L. Lovely

I believe in God, a power greater than myself. This enables me to maintain a sense of self, guides me to

the right people when I need support, and helps me
to make decisions and maintain my lifestyle.

—Marion L. Napper

God is my affirmation that the universe and life
have some principle of coherence and rationality.
God epitomizes my faith that, despite the tragedies
of personal life and the unavailability of any final
answers, life is tremendously worth living and the
heart of reality eminently sound.

—Arthur Foote

God is not an all-determining creator. Each crea-
ture is self-creating in relationship with all other
creatures, including God. So we are co-creators
with the Divine. We make God, as much as God
makes us.

—Rebecca Parker

The human and divine connection is what the
church is always all about. Individually and collec-
tively we need that connection. Our name Unitarian
reminds us that we seek to unite. Our name Univer-
salist reminds us that we seek to be complete. Never
need we be isolated; never need we be insulated. By
connecting with each other and connecting with the
divine, we feel a deeper and very special kind of
warmth. Its radiation can change our lives and can
transform our world.

—Christopher Raible

Feminist/womanist theology tries to remember the
one forgotten or intentionally left out, and recover-
ing her memory, to celebrate her life and our com-
mon life. The goddesses, Tamar, Hagar, the Un-
named Woman, the Daughter of Jephthah, the

144

Women of the Early Church, the Women at Jesus'
tomb, the mystics, the women in the nineteenth and
twentieth centuries of our own church tradition,
Frances Ellen Watkins-Harper, the Unsung Heroes,
our mothers, the Stranger, the Other, "the mad-
woman in the attic": These and more we memorial-
ize.

—Dianne E. Arakawa

For all who see God, may God go with you. For all
who embrace life, may life return you affection. For
all who seek a right path, may a way be found...and
the courage to take it, step by step.

—Robert Mabry Doss

As we are "some," God is "all" and "more." God
embraces all that has been and is, and is active
within every occasion of experience (and within
us)—luring existence toward transformation, to-
ward the beauty of what it may yet be. This is there-
fore a universe of creativity, novelty, and risk. Its
destiny is wholly open. We are partners in a divine
adventure.

—Margaret Keip

We are all theologians. We touch the running water
and the rocks. We hurt. We laugh. We grasp and
are grasped. We fall and are embraced. Broken and
fragmented, we are driven toward wholeness. Long
before we hold any belief about it, we feel the pres-
ence of something sacred and meaningful. Unable
to name it, we respond with metaphor, with vision,
with decision; and we live as though that were the
way the world is. Your theology is your commit-

ment. In Unitarian Herman Melville's words, "it is not down in any map; true places never are."

—Raymond Baughan

It is doubtful that Unitarian Universalists will ever return to a theistic claim to obey God's authority. But it is essential to our growth and future as a movement that we reclaim the passionate spirit of our predecessors, that we act in response to something Ultimate that demands our loyalty, draws us forward and gives us meaning.

—Sarah York

It is popularly supposed that between those who use the word God and those who do not there is a great gulf. But the gulf lies elsewhere. It lies between those who dogmatize, either positively or negatively, and those who recognize in great humility that something within them bears witness to realities which may be momentous in our lives, but which lie beyond the grasping net of our categories of thought. Dogmatic theism and dogmatic atheism both spring from precisely the same root, a claim that there can be strict proofs when all we can in fact see are some glimpses of majestic scenery through rifts in the enveloping clouds.

—Phillip Hewitt

Any teaching about "God" before the age of ten causes children to waste their wonderful gift of curiosity on asking questions that are not about their first-hand, unadulterated experience, but about this mysterious word...questions such as "Who made God?"

—Edith Hunter

When I am asked if I believe in God, I am either impatient or amused and frequently decline to reply. All I know, all I want to know is that I have found in my relations with others and in my glad beholding of the universe a reality of truth, goodness, and beauty and that I am trying to make my life as best I can dedication to this reality.

—John Haynes Holmes

For, if God is One, we are one with God and with one another in the universe. For me, these are the true and logical meanings of the words, Unitarian and Universalist.

—Yvonne Seon

God is that power which is both not ourselves and yet is within ourselves, which makes for righteousness. The universe is on the side of truth and justice.

—Clarence Skinner

Awe is the sense of utter dependence upon that nourishing mystery of being within which we live. We may forget this mystery, to our impoverishment, but there is no separation from it. It is given.

—Alice Blair Wesley

But I do believe that I am—that all of us are—part and parcel of a creative transcendent principle which can be called by many names. I am persuaded that the religious task is to recognize and come into harmony with our own divinity. As such, the idea of a cosmic game of hide-and-seek involving us and the creative, transcendent principle is a useful and fascinating model. It has mythic possibilities.

—William Houlff

We've all seen reproductions of the painting of God in the Sistine Chapel. What we need now is new paintings, like one of Christa, a naked, female Christ dying on the cross. She is white, but she could as easily be black, Hispanic, Asian. But even this is not enough. To shatter an image, we must confront it with a radically different one. We need mother, lover, friend. We need the washerwoman God who cleans us with her waters; the child God who is delighted with what we do; the gambler God who enjoys surprises. We need all the gods and goddesses who reveal truths for all the peoples of the world. Theology is done by humans for humans. We're the ones who construct the God-images. Our job now is to give those images meaning for our time.

—Barbara Stevens

I am an atheist. It's hard to say this without sounding either boastful or apologetic, and I don't mean to be either. Although it's not part of the usual definition of atheism, I believe all our actions, words, and thoughts affect the structure of the universe. Our effect may be vanishingly small, but when many people act or think in unison, the effect is multiplied many times.

—Henry Stone

So, yes, my God would survive WW III...even if the human race didn't survive. In the larger picture, we can't possibly destroy God, only what God we know...though that is sad enough certainly and worth working to avoid. If somehow we and our planet are a part of an infinitely flexible but inexorable plan, then we can maim the divine cause terribly but we cannot terminate it. We may resist, circumvent, delay, ignore, use our free will for-almost-

ever, but finally, I believe, there is God and that God is good, and nothing can prevent our final participation in the God.

—Christine Robinson

I believe in God, but I don't believe God cares about us...God doesn't watch or know us. God has no eyes to see, no mind to know, except in the sense that you and I have eyes and minds and we are a part of God. And since we are a very limited part, mostly God is blind and unthinking.

—Ricky Hoyt

If a radio reporter ever came to my home, I would say that God is the creative force that has cast each of us into this world. God is the love in and between people. God does not willfully direct hurricanes onto the beaches of the unjust. God is the moral conscience that demands we walk these beaches hand-in-hand, building together where hurricanes have destroyed.

—Jane Mauldin

You can believe in your heart of hearts, in the truest depths of your soul, in the clearest reckoning of your mind, that there is no god, no supernatural being or cosmic creator, and stand as good a chance as anyone else of being a good, trustworthy, loving person, and indeed, a deeply religious one. And as a Unitarian Universalist, you needn't pretend you believe otherwise.

—Ken Sawyer

Like the God, the Goddess can also be recognized as metaphor and still have great influence in our lives. The Goddess reminds us that women are as

*divine as men. The Goddess is a symbol of the One
Who Was Before. The Matrix of the Universe is an
all-encompassing creative, fertile potential, the
source of Being. In other words, the Ground of Being is a feminine symbol.*

—Sydney Wilde

*Freedom resides in every discrete entity in the uni-
verse: in atoms and cells and our own identities we
call selves. What is created is not god. What creates
is god. God is a verb, not a noun. All the world is
not god. God is an active indwelling presence.*

—Roy Reynolds

*I'm standing in line at the Registry of Motor Vehi-
cles—a long line—to renew my license, and I'm
reading some God-book or other and the guy ahead
of me in line asks me if I'm a minister and I say
"yes" and he says, "Do you believe in God?"...The
truth is, there are a lot of gods out there I don't believe in. And a few that I do believe in. So I said to
the man in line, "I believe in big mysteries. I believe
in depth of feeling—feelings so deep within the
spirit that the connection, or the bliss, or the peace,
stay with us forever. And I believe in a goodness
created by our lives and our care." He said, "Fine."
That was all there was to it, and I went back to my
book.*

—Jane R. Rzepka

*Thus, God really is love, without cavil or inconsis-
tency. In whatever sense a social being can be absolute and independent, God may be absolute and independent—but in that sense only; and in whatever
sense a social being must, in principle and therefore*

even in the ideal case, dependent upon others, God is in that sense dependent and relative.

—Charles Hartshorne

My theology supports the belief that because God is intimately interconnected within every particle of the universe, then we must embody the best of that divine quality. It is impossible for those of us who profess to believe in such an ultimate reality to simply shrug our collective shoulders and walk away.

—Betty Stapleford

The Creative Force may be understood as the power constantly at work within life and the world for goodness, truth, wholeness, and beauty. Such a God does not interfere with human freedom or the functioning of the natural world.

—William Murry

Resource List of UU Books

I have compiled the following list of books authored by Unitarian Universalists directly on or related to the theme of God. I have not chosen to annotate this particular bibliography since most of these volumes are already described in current Unitarian Universalist catalogues.

Understandably, this list is not exhaustive, but aspires to include a range of theological discourse, comprising volumes that are published in recent associational history and readily available at UUA headquarters.

Furthermore, there also exists a bounty of UU pamphlets, essays, sermons concerning a lover's quarrel with God, but such writings are scattered hither and yon; hence, I leave the sleuthing job to curious readers.

Beach, George Kimmel. *If Yes Is the Answer*. Boston: Skinner House, 1995.

Buehrens, John A., editor. *Return to the Springs: Essays and Sermons on Religious Renewal* by Jacob Trapp. Boston: Skinner House, 1987.

Campbell, Fred. *Religious Integrity for Everyone: Functional Theology for Secular Society*. Lincoln, Nebraska: Writers Club Press, 2000.

Church, Forrester. *God and Other Famous Liberals*. New York: Simon and Schuster, 1991.

Clark, John Ruskin. *The Great Living System: The Religion Emerging from the Sciences*. Boston: Skinner House, 1984.

Cohen, Helen. *Believing in Evolution*. Lexington, Massachusetts: First Parish Church, 1994.

Cummins, John. This *Strange and Wondrous Journey*. Minneapolis: Rising Press, 1991.

Fleck, G. Peter. *The Mask of Religion*. New York: Prometheus Books, 1980.

Ford, James Ishmael. *This Very Moment: Introduction to Zen Buddhism for Unitarian Universalists*. Boston: Skinner House, 1996.

Greeley, Roger, editor. *The Best of Humanism*. New York: Prometheus, 1988.

Houff, William. *Infinity in Your Hand: A Guide for the Spiritually Curious*. Spokane: Melior Publications, 1989.

Howlett, Duncan. *The Critical Way in Religion: Testing and Questing*. New York: Prometheus Books, 1980.

Jones, William. *Is God a White Racist? A Preamble to Black Theology*. Boston: Beacon Press, 1998.

Kitchell, Webster. *God's Dog: Conversations with Coyote*. Boston: Skinner House, 1992.

Mendelsohn, Jack. *Being Liberal in an Illiberal Age*. Boston: Skinner House, 1995.

Muir, Fredric John. *A Reason for Hope: Liberation Theology Confronts a Liberal Faith*. Carmel, California: Sunflower Ink, 1994.

Murry, William. *A Faith for All Seasons: Liberal Religion and the Crises of Life*. Bethesda, Maryland: River Road Press, 1990.

Olds, Mason. *Religious Humanism in America: Dietrich, Reese and Potter*. New York: University Press of America, 1978.

Papa, Stephan. *An Agnostic Talks to God*. Denver: Castle Press, 1989.

Patton, Kenneth L. *A Religion of Realities: A Philosophy of Religion*. New Jersey: Meeting House Press, 1977.

Ranck, Shirley. *Cakes for the Queens of Heaven: An Exploration of Women's Power—Past, Present, and Future*. San Diego: Delphi Press, 1995.

Schulz, William. *Finding Time and Other Delicacies*. Boston: Skinner House, 1992.

Sewell, Marilyn. *Wanting Wholeness, Being Broken: A Book of Sermons*. Portland, Oregon: Fuller Press, 1998.

Southworth, Bruce. *At Home in Creativity: The Naturalistic Theology of Henry Nelson Wieman*. Boston: Skinner House, 1995.

Stackhouse, Max, editor. *On Being Human Religiously (Selected Essays in Religion and Society)* by James Luther Adams. Boston: Beacon Press, 1976.

Thandeka. *Learning to be White: Money, Race and God in America*. New York: Continuum, 1999.

Tracy, Denise, editor. *Wellsprings: Sources in Unitarian Universalist Feminism*. Oak Park, Illinois: Adelphi Resources, 1992.

Wakefield, Dan. *How Do We Know When It's God: A Spiritual Memoir*. Boston: First Back Bay Paperback, 2000.

Wesley, Alice Blair. *Myths of Time and History: A Unitarian Universalist Theology*. Newark, Delaware: Words Unlimited, Inc., 1987.

ANNOTATED BIBLIOGRAPHY

I have selected a sampler of current books by non-Unitarian Universalist authors spanning the range of our given theme—volumes for neither the inflexible believer nor the heartless cynic, but ones that speak to open-spirited riders of paradoxes. These choices attempt to juggle keen scholarship with devotional sensibility, salted with a justice-building temper. Plus, most of them are printed in paperback and quite accessible to lay readers.

Angeles, Peter A., editor. *Critiques of God: Making the Case Against Belief in God.* New York: Prometheus Books, 1997. A definitive anthology in the philosophy of religion that exclusively presents the case against God. Varied and stimulating pieces by a stable of outstanding contemporary philosophers.

Armstrong, Karen. *A History of God: The 4000-Year Quest of Judaism, Christianity and Islam.* New York: Ballantine Books, 1991. One of Britain's foremost commentators on religious affairs moves from classical philosophy and medieval mysticism to the Reformation, through the Enlightenment to our modern age of uncertainty. An encyclopedic yet engaging study of how the three dominant monotheistic religions have shaped and altered the conception of God.

Borg, Marcus J. *The God We Never Knew: Beyond Dogmatic Religion to a More Authentic Contemporary Faith.* San Francisco: HarperCollins Paperback, 1997. Best-selling Protestant theologian produces a volume that speaks to unbelieving seekers as well as struggling theists. Highly readable treatise with an especially strong section on "panentheism."

Borg, Marcus and **MacKenzie**, Ross, editors. *God at 2000*. Harrisburg, Pennsylvania: Morehouse Publishing, 2000. Seven well-known scholars, from a variety of faith perspectives, address the simple question: "From your lifetime of study, reflection, and experience, what have you learned about God or the Sacred that seems important to you?" Karen Armstrong, Marcus Borg, Joan Chittister, Diana Eck, Lawrence Kushner, Sayyed Hossein Nasr, and Desmond Tutu discuss their own unique and personal perspectives and discover that despite varied understandings, they share some common conclusions about God. A most challenging and inspirational collection.

Eck, Diana L. *Encountering God: A Spiritual Journey from Bozeman to Banaras*. Boston: Beacon Press, 1993. The Director of the Pluralism Project is a preeminent spokesperson for religious diversity in America, particularly the increasing dialogue with Hindus, Buddhists, and Muslim communities. A bridging volume that extends our standard western worldview.

Gallagher, Winifred. *Working on God*. New York: Random House, 1999. This book is composed specifically for people who are unclear and tentative about the subject of religion. The author calls them "neo-agnostics"—well-educated skeptics who have "inexplicable metaphysical feelings." A reporter of behavioral science, Gallagher ably spans the secular and religious domains through research, interviews, and personal odyssey.

Grumbach, Doris. *The Presence of Absence: On Prayers and an Epiphany*. Boston: Beacon Press, 1998. A professional writer who crafts her spiritual memoir in the lineage of Anne Lamott, Frederick Buechner, Kathleen Norris, and Simone Weil. A fearlessly honest account full of yearning, impasses, and communion.

Johnson, Elizabeth A. *She Who Is: The Mystery of God in Feminist Theological Discourse*. New York: Crossroad, 1996. A progressive Catholic scholar who struggles amidst the ultimate unknowability of the divine. She recognizes that all theological pilgrims must wrestle with this crucial question: "What is the right way to speak of God in the face of women's newly cherished human dignity and equality?" Johnson ably extends the thought of three earlier and pacesetting Beacon Press books: (1) *Beyond God the Father: Toward a Philosophy of Women's Liberation* by Mary Daly (1973); (2) *Behind the Sex of God: Toward a New Consciousness Transcending Matriarchy and Patriarchy* by Carol Ochs (1977); and (3) *Sexism and God-Talk: Toward a Feminist Theology* by Rosemary Radford Ruether (1983).

Keen, Sam. *Hymns to an Unknown God: Awakening the Spirit in Everyday Life*. New York: Bantam Books, 1994. An inspiring guide to finding and re-creating the sense of expanded meaning that so many fervently seek in today's society. The author furnishes not a set of directions toward a clearly defined end but a map to an adventure of one's own mind and heart, body and soul. Draws upon the collected wisdom of both East and West.

Kushner, Harold. *Who Needs God?* New York: Pocket Books, 1989. Reflective essays from a broad-minded Jewish perspective that speak compellingly to the emptiness of modern women and men. Useful nourishment for the soul that posits a mature faith that doesn't offend one's reason.

McDaniel, Jay B. *Of God and Pelicans: A Theology of Reverence for Life*. Louisville, Kentucky: Westminster/John Knox Press, 1989. A book that contributes toward healing our relations with animals and the rest of Earth's creation. It deals with issues of theodicy and animal rights in a life-centered perspective, using insights from feminism, process thought, and Buddhism. Well-argued and imaginative.

McFague, Sallie. *Models of God: Theology for an Ecological, Nuclear Age*. Philadelphia: Fortress Press, 1987. A progressive perspective that utilizes metaphors in an effort to clarify what is ultimately mysterious—the relationship between God and the universe. Novel and lucid models depicting God as Mother, Lover, and Friend.

Miles, Jack. *God: A Biography*. New York: Vintage Books, 1995. Using the Hebrew Bible as his text, this author unravels an evolving deity—a character who possesses immense contradictions and depths. Refreshingly combines the touch of the journalist, the knowledge of the scholar, and the regard of the dubious believer.

Moreland, J. P. and **Nielsen**, Kai. *Does God Exist? The Debate Between Theists and Atheists* with contributions by William Lane Craig, Anthony Flew, Peter Kreeft, Keith Parsons, and Dallas Willard. New York: Prometheus, 1993. Whether you are a theist, agnostic, or unbeliever your convictions will be stretched into new shapes by these philosophers addressing one of life's most fundamental questions.

Raymo, Chet. *Skeptics and True Believers: The Exhilarating Connection Between Science and Religion.* New York: Walker and Company, 1998. A resilient doubter who respects both the scientific urge to understand and the religious need to celebrate creation. A professor of physics and astronomy who displays the openness to awe and wonder of a scientifically revealed universe.

Schmidt, Frederic W., editor. *The Changing Face of God.* Harrisburg, Pennsylvania: Morehouse Publishing, 2000. Five scholars presented provocative lectures at Washington National Cathedral that addressed varied images of God and the differences these perspectives render in human experience. Contributors include Karen Armstrong, Marcus Borg, James Cone, Jack Miles, and Andrew Sung Park. A critically reverent appreciation of God.

Shield, Benjamin and **Carlson**, Richard, editors. *For the Love of God: New Writings by Spiritual and Psychological Leaders.* San Rafael, California: New World Library, 1990. A collection of 26 essays that reflect the psycho-spiritual renaissance of the late 20th century. Prominent figures from around the world discuss their personal relationship with God.

Stannard, Russell, editor. *God for the 21st Century.* Philadelphia: Templeton Foundation Press, 2000. Some 50 thinkers discuss the relationship between science and religion. Topics range from astronomy and cosmology, genetic engineering, extraterrestrial life, psychology and religious experience, spirituality and medicine to artificial intelligence—all focused on expanding our understanding of divine mystery.

Taylor, Barbara Brown. *The Luminous Web: Essays on Science and Religion*. Boston: Cowley Publications, 2000. An evocative set of lectures on the dialogue between science and religion by an Episcopal priest. Taylor seeks to uncover why scientists sometimes sound like poets and physicists use the language of imagination, ambiguity, and mystery.

Weems, Renita. *Listening for God: A Minister's Journey Through Silence and Doubt*. New York: Simon and Schuster, 1999. A guidebook for others even as it comprises private conversations with God. The author addresses all seasons of spiritual development, especially offering a beacon of light to those languishing amidst the doldrums of winter.

Questions for Personal Reflection

or Journaling

Composed by Elizabeth Motander Jones

1.   Reflect upon how your relationship to god or the divine has changed over the span of your life. Note times when you have had to wrestle with your own conflicting concepts and beliefs. Have there been any pivotal moments or events? How do you believe your family, friends, location, and education (formal and informal) have influenced you in this area?

2.   Which of the three positions, Atheism, Agnosticism, and Affirmatisim, lives in you? If more than one, do they coexist peacefully? How?

3.   Ralph Waldo Emerson is quoted—"If you believe, suspend your belief. If you doubt, take a leap of faith!" What is he asking us to do? What can taking a position different from our usual one do for us? What do we risk in doing so? What might we gain?

4.   What are your reactions to the following classifications of atheists: devoted, distracted, functional, hopeful, and pessimistic?

5.   What is your reaction to what is described as the purifying role of atheism?

6.   In looking at the sources of the word agnostic, the phrase "to stand in awe before the unknown" is used. How does this "active reverence" relate to your understanding of agnosticism?

7. How do you feel about the use of the term Affir-matisim? What does it say to you?

8. Why is it that the **location** of God might be more important to Unitarian Universalists than the **definition?**

9. Six lurking-places of God are noted—**service, stuff, silliness, struggle, silence, and surrender.** Where among these or in other places have you encountered God? If you are an atheist or an agnostic, do these "lurking places" have significance for you? What is it you find there?

10. How can the **Seven Fundamental Reminders** be of assistance to you in exploring and wrestling with your relationship to god?

Also By Tom Owen-Towle:

Generation to Generation

Staying Together

New Men: Deeper Hungers

Spiritual Fitness

Brother-Spirit

The Gospel of Universalism

Friendship Chronicles

Sauntering

Borne on a Wintry Wind

Love Meets the Dragons

Freethinking Mystics with Hands

Bridge Called Respect

Hard Blessings

Wholly Joy!

Mail Order Information:

For additional copies of *Wrestling With God* send $12.95 per book, plus $2 for shipping and handling (add 7.75% sales tax—CA residents). Make checks payable to:

Tom Owen-Towle
3303 Second Avenue
San Diego, CA 92103

Telephone: (619) 295-7067

E-mail: uutom@cox.net